PASSIONS

PASSIONS

How to Manage Despair,
Fear, Rage, and Guilt and
Heighten Your Capacity
for Joy, Love, Hope, and Awe

Dr. Georgia Witkin

Villard Books
New York 1992

Library of Congress Cataloging-in-Publication Data

Witkin, Georgia.

    Passions: how to manage despair, fear, rage, and guilt and heighten your capacity for joy, love, hope, and awe / Georgia Witkin.—1st ed.

        p.   cm.

    ISBN 0-394-57914-3

    1. Emotions. 2. Self-management (Psychology) I. Title.

BF561.W58 1992   152.4—dc20   91-50069

Manufactured in the United States of America

9 8 7 6 5 4 3 2

First edition

This book was set in 10.5/15 Meridien

Book design by Charlotte Staub

My beloved mother, Mildred—
this book is dedicated to you.

You live with passion,
you teach passion,
you inspire passion.

Never, never give up.

Acknowledgments

Diane Reverand discovered this book in my thoughts, research, and articles. Joan Lippert Indig fine-tuned this book with her editing skills, questions, ideas, and suggestions. This book is theirs as it is mine. And now we share it with you.

CONTENTS

INTRODUCTION

This is a book for the timid—for those of you who fear emotions because they can be so overwhelming.

This is a book for the numb—for all who know that passions are locked in their heart but cannot feel them.

This is a book for the skeptical—for the people who do not believe that emotions are an important part of living.

This is also a book for people who are too *familiar with life's ups and downs*—for those who are confused and exhausted by their feelings, for those who live in a constant emotional hurricane, resting only in the eye of the storm.

Emotions are our human response to life. As a practicing clinical psychologist, I can assure you that emotions need not hurt us, overwhelm us, or frighten us, but in order for this to happen, we must first understand them. In the pages that follow, we will examine the origins of eight great passions. You will learn how to master those that feel uncontrollable, survive those that make you uncomfortable, and enhance those that you enjoy.

What Makes an Emotion a Passion?

Not all strong emotions are passions. Some emotions are mainly of the mind, while others arouse the body. Amusement, confusion, and boredom are mind emotions, accompanied by very few body changes. We can ponder, wonder, and muse for hours without moving from a comfortable position in a comfortable chair. Our pupils will not dilate and our palms will not sweat. Subtle brain-wave patterns may suggest that we are contemplating rather than sleeping or leaping, but overall there are no physical telltale signs. The mind emotions may affect us for a day, but without a physical component they are not dramatic enough to change our life.

Terror and shock, on the other hand, are mainly body emotions involving major body-state changes. Our heart rate can double, as can our rate of respiration. We may flush as peripheral blood vessels dilate, then feel chilled or numb after body heat is lost. As for the mind, it can seem to stop functioning altogether—frozen with terror or disoriented by shock. The body emotions, such as terror and shock, are vivid but short-lived, since the body cannot sustain such effects for long.

It is those peak emotions that seize both the mind *and* body, however, that we remember as the extraordinary ones. They are full experiences and we participate in them totally. They are mentally obsessing and physically possessing. They are the emotions that texture our memories and even change our lives. They are too intense to last. They always pass. We call them passions.

Eight Great Passions
Love

Love is the "passion" everybody thinks of first, but many of its forms are not passions. Friendship and affection, for example, are forms of love, but they are mainly of the mind. Lust, on the other hand, is an emotion that is mainly of the body. The passionate love I am referring to is the most powerful love, a passion of both the mind and body. When we are passionately in love, we adore the object of our love and constantly think about him or her. We feel physical sensations even if the relationship is not a sexual one. We yearn to touch our beloved, body and soul. The adage is to fall in love—passionate love makes one feel like we are falling off a cliff, an uncontrollable yet tantalizing and exhilarating fall. Passionate love is the great love we all hope we will find one day. If we have already found such passion, we hope it will never go away. Although love can grow, its peaks can only be temporary (as we will see is the case with all of the passions). Passionate love is an experience that can return again and again, and it is an experience we never forget.

Joy

As with passionate love, joy increases our heart rate and respiration, dilates our blood vessels, and relaxes our muscles as the body floods with *endorphins*, happiness hormones. In my research I have identified eleven types of joy:

- the joy of love
- the joy of triumph
- the joy of mastery
- the joy of surprise
- the joy of safety
- the joy of reprieve
- the joy of another's joy
- the joy of positive anticipation
- the joy of extraordinary experience
- the joy of laughter
- the joy of faith

In my research I have found that joys do not come and go as whimsically as we have thought. Joy comes most frequently and steadily to those who create opportunities for joy. Soon you will learn how to create your own opportunities.

Rage

Not all passions are positive; some we call negative passions. When we feel passionately angry, we call it rage. When we are enraged, the action hormone *adrenaline* alerts our body and fires us up for the fight-or-flight response. In rage, we sometimes choose the fight option—we yell, we throw, we pound, or shake with rage as we try to control it. Sometimes we choose the flight option—we slam doors behind us as we leave a room, home, or even a life we have created for ourselves. Regrets may follow, but only after the powerful passion has ebbed.

Fear

In fear, we also experience the fight-or-flight response. Fear, like rage, makes us uncomfortable; while the dramatic mind/body response may have been useful to our primitive *ancestors*, it seems to interfere in our temperature-controlled, safety-latched lives of today. Yet the fright response is still an important part of survival and communication; terror can help us run from an attacker on the street, fight for our children when our own survival is threatened, and freeze wordlessly until danger is past.

Guilt

You perspire, your stomach knots, you have trouble sleeping, and you relive in your mind the thing you did or did not do. You cannot laugh, you cannot eat, and you cannot escape that small voice of shame and blame in your head that makes you feel very, very uncomfortable. It is possible to feel so guilty that it becomes a passion. Children suffer from guilt when they do something "bad," something they *should not* do. Adults suffer from guilt when they fail to do something "good," something they *should* do. This passion is primitive, persistent, and powerful.

Despair

Despair begins with an event, most often a loss: a job, a friend, our health. Sad thoughts leave us feeling melancholy, washed out, and unable to move. It is despair you feel when you give up on the world. Depression makes us feel helpless; despair makes us feel hopeless. But despair is "grief in brief." Like all passions, thankfully (in this case), it passes.

Hope

We can wait for despair to go away by itself or we can create its antidote, hope. Hope goes beyond mere wanting. Our minds become alert and our bodies energized. When we hope, the vision before our eyes is so real that we may actually reach out to it, taking the first steps toward it and fulfilling our own desire.

Awe

A magnificent sight or a spectacular accomplishment fills us with a sense that life has greatness and meaning, and we stand still with respect and admiration. When that which we perceive is so magnificent or spectacular that it makes us feel very small, awe is tinged with fear. When what we perceive is so fleeting or minute that we feel very enlarged, awe is tinged with gratitude.

Prisoners of the Heart

I have found that peak emotions can make us uncomfortable. This goes for positive passions, such as joy, love, hope, and awe, as well as for the negative passions of despair, rage, guilt, and fear. Why? The men and women of all ages who were interviewed for this book, and for my three previous books tell me that positive passions seem to be too fleeting and their end too painful, while the negative ones are too frightening. Consequently, they try to run from them, avoid them, and deny them.

We develop elaborate excuses for our emotional detachment. We say being emotional uses up time: "I could spend an hour sitting on the porch appreciating the sunset, but the house is a mess." We say that emotion immobilizes us: "I could take a day to lie down and grieve, but who will make dinner?"

We say we do not want to act on our emotions because we are afraid of exposure, of being judged, of revealing too much: "Will everyone think I'm ridiculous if I cry for joy when I take communion?" Or, "I don't want him to leave, but what if I make a scene in the airport?"

We say emotions are too costly, even the positive ones: "If I enjoy happiness now, I'll pay a bill in sorrow later." So instead, we don't act on our positive emotions—we do not allow ourselves to feel joy, love, hope, and wonderment. We block the intensity of what we feel.

We say we fear retribution for negative emotions: "But the other person will be emotional right back, at an intensity I can't handle!" Or, "If I show her my anger, she'll never let me forget it."

We say emotions leave us vulnerable: "If I let myself fall in love, will I be rejected again?" We tell ourselves that in our competitive world, a show of emotion will be interpreted as a show of weakness, which may be used against us later.

Both overpassionate and timid people sometimes fall into the habit of hiding feelings they think are inappropriate. My Passions Survey of men and women revealed a good deal of deception at work when it comes to what we feel compared with what we allow others to see.

THE EMOTIONS WE HIDE

%	Fear	Jealousy	Despair	Anxiety	Anger	Guilt	Infatuation	Rage	Love	Contentment
21	x	x								
	x	x								
18	x	x	x							
	x	x	x							
15	x	x	x							
	x	x	x							
12	x	x	x							
	x	x	x	x	x					
9	x	x	x	x	x					
	x	x	x	x	x	x				
6	x	x	x	x	x	x				
	x	x	x	x	x	x	x	x		
3	x	x	x	x	x	x	x	x		
	x	x	x	x	x	x	x	x	x	x

The most hidden emotions were fear and jealousy. Despair was close behind, with other negative emotions trailing at a distance. Survey respondents included more than four hundred men and women— secretaries, housewives, entrepreneurs, physicians, psychologists, students, teachers, bankers, musicians, retired people, and more— who each chose these emotions from a list of thirteen possibilities as the ones they try to hide from other people.

Are You Numb or Skeptical?

If you have become so estranged from your emotions that you feel numb, you are not alone. If you imagine that enormous passions lie locked in your heart and you cannot feel them now, you are not alone. People who are timid often become numb in time; so do people whose most frequent emotions express pain. Some of us end up living so apart from our emotions that we deny them completely. When I asked men and women which emotion they *never* felt, these are the ones they came up with most often:

THE EMOTIONS WE DENY

%	Infatuation	Despair	Rage	Contentment	Courage	Jealousy	Anxiety	Hope
22	x							
20	x	x						
18	x	x	x					
16	x	x	x	x				
14	x	x	x	x				
12	x	x	x	x				
10	x	x	x	x				
8	x	x	x	x	x	x		
6	x	x	x	x	x	x		
4	x	x	x	x	x	x	x	
2	x	x	x	x	x	x	x	x

Infatuation and despair were the peak emotions that the most people in the Passions Survey said they never feel. Nearly as many said they have no rage or contentment in their lives. No rule says every person must feel every emotion, but can our lives be so static that we *never* experience infatuation, despair, rage, or blissful contentment? Many psychologists and psychiatrists know that denial can mean its opposite: the emotion denied is actually frightening or confusing, and denial is an attempt to push the emotion back into Pandora's box. No one denied feeling anger, however, and almost no one denied feeling guilt, joy, or love. These are the emotions we speak of easily. These are the emotions of daily life. It was encouraging to find that many people did not have any answer at all to the survey question, "I never feel . . ." Perhaps this says that many people are not only experiencing a full range of emotions, but they are also aware of them.

Emotions or Else?

Maybe you expect me to say that something *terrible* happens when you hold emotions in, that you explode emotionally later on or are creating diseases, ulcers, or even cancer. While emotions have been proven to make waves in the body's immune system, I believe that they cannot play a role without viruses, bacteria, and genetics. And saying that emotions directly cause diseases and disorders encourages us to blame ourselves when we are already ailing—a sad and, I believe, inaccurate thought. Emotions may indeed affect our health through our immune system, but emotions are not pollutants or poisons. They are not medicines, either. Perfect, positive passions cannot, unfortunately, guarantee longevity. Randomness, humanness, and our capacities and limits, our decisions and our hesitations, will also determine our fate.

Being impassioned is not, therefore, a death threat. Nor is being passionless life-threatening. About the worst thing that can happen when we try to suppress our passions is that we send them off at an angle, changing their original direction. But being without passion is more of a regret. If you feel passionless, consider yourself an emotional virgin who has much beauty, wisdom, and richness to experience in your life ahead.

Packaged Passions

The value of the passions is in the texture they give to each day and night we live. Without them, we often turn to packaged passions to get some emotional spice into our life when our own passions seem numbed. A bit of release and expression, a short emotional adventure, and then we are again as we were before.

Television tune-in Television is a passion substitute available at the press of a button.

> Rose is fifty-two years old and satisfied, she says, with her life. Her husband is retired and busy with hobbies. Her son and two daughters are married and successful; she sees them often. In between, she sews, practices calligraphy . . . and spends four hours a day watching soap operas. She identifies with one character on each of the shows and enters that person's life for half an hour each day. Rose's explanation is that these shows teach her what not to do—"I can't believe the mess these people make of their lives!" she says. This position of wisdom and safety makes Rose feel more content about leading a life with few emotional ups and downs.

Rose is unaware of it, but the soaps are her safe substitute for passions, for emotions she dares not express. Occasionally, for just a moment, she finds herself thinking that her life is unbearably boring. Her husband belittles her, and he has forbidden her to look for work outside the home. When she thinks about this, it makes her feel powerless, uncomfortably dependent and, sometimes, enraged. Expressing her feelings directly could threaten the stability of her marriage. So for Rose, the soaps provide escape to another world and allow her to vicariously experience passions that, in her everyday world, she does without.

The sound of passion   Teenagers enjoy living in vicarious worlds too: They watch MTV, for example, endlessly. Tune in for half an hour, and you will see the enormous range of emotions these videos dramatize. You will see lust, loneliness, guilt, anger, beauty both human and in nature, love and love lost, pain, despair, hope, and, in the dance moves, uninhibited joy!

Music has always been a way people can express or feel passion. What are your favorite songs? What lines, especially, do you catch yourself head-humming most often? If you take a minute when you catch yourself humming, you may be surprised to find that music is a good barometer of your mood. Pay attention to the words of the song you are singing in your head if you want a clue to the feelings inside you. The recording industry knows this. The peak emotions keep the entertainment business in business.

The arts   The energy used by the artist in the act of creation is emotional energy—and we can feel its heat whenever we draw close. Consider, for example, this tale. It is a classic example of passion as an art form.

Carmen is beautiful, single, and a compulsive flirt. The men who thrill her most are the ones with an air of danger. Recently, though, her beauty has attracted a very stable, though somewhat boring army man named Joe. She encourages him, and he follows her around to the point that he fails to meet his responsibilities in the service and is dishonorably discharged. Now the infatuated Joe is desperate. He has time on his hands and intensifies his efforts to win Carmen. He is crazed with love. He challenges and fights with one of her other boyfriends, but Carmen is not impressed. She is getting tired of him and decides to get rid of him. It is all too much for Joe. One night Carmen appears in public on the arm of a wealthy local businessman. Joe cannot bear it and threatens her with a knife.

As you may have guessed, the anecdote above is an opera plot, slightly modernized—it is *Carmen*, by Georges Bizet, first performed in 1875. Besides loneliness, guilt, anger, and love, operatic productions and plays deliver hellish grief and deep despair, murderous rage, and jealous, possessive love to end all love.

And other fine arts are also about peak emotions. The ballet is often a paean to erotic love and the beauty of the human body. Paintings and sculptures express the sagas of their creators.

But though the act of artistic creation may be passionate, the act of appreciation is typically more passive. We can stand back and criticize, analyze, process, and praise. We are mere voyeurs while the artists bare their essence. Artistic appreciation is a channel for experiencing emotions that is 100 percent approved by our society—and 100 percent safe for the user.

Passion between the covers   Go into any bookstore and you will see long racks full of paperbacks with the same thing on the cover: a man and a woman locked in an embrace, or close to it. Just looking at the cover is supposed to make you yearn to know what is inside. I will tell you. In these books, people act on every emotion they feel: love, hate, joy, grief, tenderness, rage, hope, despair, daring, fear, jealousy, guilt . . .

Whatever has ever happened to anyone can usually be found in one of these romance novels, probably by the end of the first chapter. What a self-indulgent luxury it would be to live the way these storybook men and women do! How well they must sleep at night, with so little turmoil left within their heaving breasts. Millions of readers, mostly women, take time out from their own very practical lives to vicariously experience the passions of heroines.

Passions rule some of our best literature as well. Terror, horror, good humor, long laughs, fury, throbbing hearts and trembling lips—they are standard fare. Consider for example, Fyodor Dostoyevsky's *Crime and Punishment*. The book is a study of emotions, of unconscious thoughts that constantly come to the surface. It is a complex interplay of desire, control, action, and confession. Any time we think our own life is lacking in passion, we can get a vicarious dosage in these pages or those of many other classics.

I am not even hinting, however, that we stop reading. I am suggesting that we also start an emotional life of our own that is worthy of retelling, rich in feeling and unique in style. I am saying that it is time to animate our days, vitalize our nights, and let our biography write itself with vigor.

Are You Overpassionate?

Though emotions tell the tale of our inner life, it is not healthier to live in constant turmoil than it is to be emotionally numb. Consider Lydia:

Lydia is twenty years old and, from the outside, seems to have finances under control. She has a million dollars from her father's estate. But she told me she cannot get control over her spending. She feels terror as she watches money flow through her fingers, and she cannot seem to grasp control any more than she could grasp water.

From the outside, her life seems to be aglitter with parties and friends, but to Lydia her social life feels like opportunities for disaster. Lydia told me of a fancy fund-raising gala and then of her impulsive decision to walk alone, dressed in a long gown and fur coat, through the streets of New York at 2 A.M. A street person snatched her evening bag, she barely escaped rape, and she has cried every day since.

From the outside, Lydia's future seems rosy. Lydia is involved with a bright, intelligent, caring man she is sure she will marry. But in an irresponsible moment she still cannot explain, she decided not to "bother" with her diaphragm. This led to an abortion last month, about which she is still confused.

Lydia loves living life with gusto, but even she recognizes that she is generating agitation and confusing aggravation with vitality.

Lydia's life resounds with echoes of an emotionally abusive past and an overly emotional present. The only time she is at peace is when a passion has exhausted her.

If you are constantly emotionally overwrought like Lydia, it is time to sort out your feelings. Constant ups and downs may be your protection against feelings of boredom or of being boring. Experiencing an emotional roller coaster may be a sign that you are taking too much of life far too personally. It may mean that you are hypomanic—that is, you are trying to ward off depression, which is a lack of feeling, by having too many feelings. Or you may be experiencing an agitated depression—hyperactivity, premenstrual syndrome, biochemical or other hormonal imbalances. If you have not reached your own diagnosis, a professional will be able to help you bring down the curtain on a string of overly dramatic roles.

You may sometimes feel that passions simply overtake you and that you cannot resist them—that is why you need to examine your passions. You probably hold more power to shape your passions than you think, and this book will help you learn many ways of doing it. Remember, most of us have some problem with our passions. Both the emotional virgin and the overly emotional need to know that our *capacity* for peak emotions is innate, their expression is often vital, and their suppression usually futile. Since they stir us up, excite us, and even agitate us, we often look at them as an inconvenient disorder, like a nasty bout of the flu. In reality, emotions can be goal-directed, activating, and expressive. Without emotions, life becomes a dull routine or an intellectual exercise. But with emotions, life is a journey of self-discovery.

THE PASSIONS SURVEY

Perhaps now is a good time for me to interview you about your deepest emotions. I have found that many of us want to talk about our emotions, but we rarely have the chance. This unquenched desire became apparent to me after *Health Magazine* published my four-part series several years ago on the peak emotions: "Joy," "Infatuation," "Rage," and "Despair." At the end of the articles I invited readers to write to me with questions and experiences—and they did! They poured out their hearts. From their letters as well as from interviews with friends, acquaintances, and patients, I gathered the anecdotes you will see throughout this book and shaped the "Passions Survey," the multi-question fill-in sheet you see reprinted on the following page.

The Passions Survey respondents included more than four hundred women and men. For more than five years I found them across the country in lecture halls; in women's health centers, hospitals, universities, and corporations where I speak or teach. Because the respondents volunteered to take the survey, it cannot be called a random sample. But it is a representative sample, including people from all walks of life. Ages ranged from eighteen to sixty-three years; some were divorced or separated, the rest about evenly divided between married and single. I encouraged the respondents to be honest in their responses by allowing them to fill in the questionnaire anonymously.

Now it is your turn to take the survey. Then compare your responses to those of others as you read the pages that follow.

PASSIONS SURVEY

Complete each of the first seven sentences with one of these emotions:

love	despair	infatuation	joy
contentment	jealousy	anxiety	hope
courage	guilt	rage	fear
	anger		

1. I most often feel _____.
2. My most intense feeling is _____.
3. My favorite feeling is _____.
4. I am most uncomfortable when I feel _____.
5. I am most uncomfortable when others express _____.
6. I never feel _____.
7. I try to hide my feelings of _____.

Complete the following:
I have felt my greatest joy when _____.
I feel rage when _____.
What I fear most is _____.
I am most despairing when _____.
My definition of love is _____.
I feel perfect contentment when _____.
I show my love by _____.
I become jealous when _____.
I generate hope by _____.
My most intense guilt is about _____.
My greatest source of anxiety is _____.
My idea of courage is _____.
When I am infatuated, my most notable change is _____.
_____.
_____.
_____.
_____.

PASSIONS

A PASSION IS BORN

Emotions seem to overtake us. "I don't know what came over me!" we say. We wonder where the emotion came from and why it arrived so suddenly.

If you think *you* have been overwhelmed by your emotions, imagine what it is like to a child. Delay lunch and the baby who is hungry cries despairingly as if the end of the world were at hand. Twirl the mobile over the child's crib and the baby's bright eyes fill with wonderment. Step out of the room, and your infant will shriek in fear; return and you are greeted with limitless love. Take a toy from a child's hands and you see rage of an intensity rare in adults. All of this is just in one *hour* in a baby's life! No wonder they are exhausted by 7 P.M. No wonder their parents are exhausted, also.

Baby's First Emotion

Did you know that our capacity for emotion is innate? A three-day-old baby can imitate a happy, sad, or surprised face. This early receptiveness to others' emotions seems to have a purpose. We convey through our facial expressions what we think of the child and that is what the child learns to think of himself. This is why so many child-development experts place enormous emphasis on a child's earliest days and weeks. They believe that the child whose capacity for imitation is stimulated early will grow up to be a more expressive adult and will probably be better at interacting emotionally with other people than a child who has not been given so much feedback.

During the first week of life, a baby also discovers one of the first emotion of her own that she can express: distress. Think about a baby who was last fed three hours ago. The distinctive whimpering or wailing sounds she makes are distress signals. The opposite of distress is another primary emotion, contentment, the one we see at the other end of the feeding schedule, when the baby's stomach is full. The infant then is so relaxed and satisfied that she can fall asleep in your arms.

At three months infants have found a new emotion, delight, and they use it to explore the world around them. Their pleasure in a soft patchwork ball or a stuffed animal with a simple face is obvious in their bright eyes and smile. Delight makes the experience of reaching out interesting and rewarding, so the child does it again and again and learns about his world.

By six months, a child is practicing her capacity for fear. She can tell an unfamiliar face from a familiar one and shows a definite preference for the one she knows. The stranger can frighten her, and she cries and flails in order to get away. And at this point of development the baby has discovered anger. She screams and gets redder in the face than would seem imaginable.

Sometime between nine and twelve months comes elation. A child this age can clap and squeal as his eyes open wide at the sight of soap bubbles in the air. Elation makes a child's first birthday a party for both the child and his parents.

By thirteen months, a toddler is often totally terrified of strangers, but she can be won over because she has learned about affection.

There is nothing like a small child's affection! Those warm, soft hands clutching your neck, the little nose buried in your hair as you hug . . . This is the age when children begin to give precious gifts to us: a pretty pebble, a dandelion.

By eighteen months, the child knows jealousy. Bringing a new baby into a home where a toddler this age or older already lives is an emotional encounter. The older sibling may regress to earlier behavior. He may have trouble sleeping or may forget his toilet training. He may show his jealousy overtly by trying to hurt the younger baby or direct his anger at other targets.

By twenty-four months, a child is ready for full-fledged joy. She jumps, claps, laughs, and runs around. Her happiness can be so physical that she looks like she might fly away.

Two researchers, Bretherton and Beeghly, who listened to a group of twenty-eight-month-old children, heard these words more often than others: *love, like, mad, scared, happy,* and *sad.* Children not only have the capacity to experience emotions, but they can put a name to their experience. Note that two emotions we do not see in children this age and younger are guilt and hope. These differ from the others because they call for intellectual maturity, self-knowledge, and an understanding of a future time and place. Readiness for these two emotions usually develops around five years of age.

But anyone who takes care of infants knows that even though they may have the same capacity for the basic emotions, emotional *temperaments* or *styles* vary enormously. For decades, mothers have used two simple words to describe this: easy or difficult. The easy baby is cheerful, cuddly, smiles a lot, looks around with interest, and does not object much to anything. The difficult baby cries, whines, and rages—and ignores you if you try to comfort her! A child psychologist, however, might categorize babies more scientifically: hyper-excitable and hypo-arousable. The hyper-excitable baby seems irritable a lot of the time. Her muscles are tense, she pulls away from people who try to hold her (even her mother), and she shrieks. The hypo-arousable baby is quite the opposite: He hardly reacts to touch, sight, or sound at all.

In the sixties and seventies, researchers would have traced such temperamental differences between children to the way we parents, mostly mothers, interacted with them. What a lot of guilt we accepted! If our child was a little bit introverted or unfriendly, we allowed ourselves to be convinced that it was because of something we had done. Even autism, the emotional disorder in which a child seems to be living in his own world, was said to be our fault. But now we suspect that genetic predispositions play a part in how extroverted, how motivated for achievement, how conscientious, and how energized we are.

Research with identical twins also confirms that some of our emotional temperaments is due to nature not nurture. Identical twins have identical genetic potential. If they are raised apart, therefore, differences are likely to be due to environment (nurture), and similarities are most likely inheritance (nature). When psychologist Thomas J. Bouchard of the University of Minnesota polled twins who had been separated at a young age and reared apart, he found striking similarities in their scores on some measures of temperament: leadership ability, traditionalism, and irritability. Other researchers have found that identical twins who are reared apart are also concordant (more like their twin than the families they grew up with) for sleepwalking, car sickness, nail-biting, vulnerability to alcoholism, bedwetting and sweating under stress!

If some temperament is innate, then the wisest and least frustrating course of action you can take is to try to get to know your child as early as you can. Rather than try to change your child or create your child, help your child learn to know himself and know how to live with himself.

So far, only one trait seems to be all nurture. Robert Plomin, a developmental psychologist at Pennsylvania State University, has concluded that early environment has more to do with niceness than genetic heritage does. Niceness, meaning how trusting, sympathetic, and cooperative—or cynical, callous, and antagonistic—you are. But even this characteristic, I suspect, probably begins with a natural predisposition that gets encouraged by nice parents.

One role of nurture, then, is to stimulate, reinforce, demonstrate, and elaborate on that which our nature has to offer. An important part of nurture is your cultural heritage. Our ancestors brought foods, fashions, and festivals, but according to social psychologists, all cultural groups also brought *emotional* traditions, ranging from exuberance to dourness. Now that we are all working and playing together, of course, many of our emotional traditions are blending. But we still learn many emotional scripts young and never rewrite them. In the years to come, as traditions mix through marriage and remarriage, and as children's scripts are written by television as well as tradition, we can expect to see a new American emotionality.

The Emotion Experts and Their Explanations

Webster's dictionary traces the word "emotion" back to the Latin *emovere*. "e" means "out," and "movere" means "move"—in other words, an expression outward *from* oneself.

But we usually think of an emotion as something that happens *to* oneself. We think of our self as taken over and victimized by strong emotions. In fact, the word "passion" comes from the same Latin root as passive! Philosopher R. C. Solomon in his book *The Passions* (Anchor/Doubleday, Garden City, N.Y. 1976) suggests that perhaps we want to seem passive so that we won't be held responsible for our emotional behavior:

- we "fall in" love
- we are "paralyzed" by fear
- we are "plagued" by remorse
- we are "undone" by jealousy
- we are "distracted" by grief
- we are "haunted" by guilt
- we are "driven" to anger

Are we really "struck" by an emotion, as if by a car? Are we really "overwhelmed" by sadness or "overcome" by rage? Do we have to wait for emotions to happen to us? The answer seems to be "No!"

One of the first formal explanations of emotion was the James-Lange theory, formulated at the end of the last century. William James, an American psychologist, and Carl Lange, a Danish physiologist, independently reached the conclusion that emotions begin with the body not the mind. For example, according to their theory, first we find ourselves crying and then know we are sad. Common sense says we meet a bear, are frightened, and run, but Lange suggests that we meet a bear, run, and then feel fear. Can we first smile and then feel happier? Today some researchers again say "Yes." And they recommend just that.

Just before the depression of the 1930s, neurologist Walter B. Cannon and his colleague Philip Bard speculated that the bodily response and the sensation of emotion happen *together*. Bard and Cannon pointed to the brain's thalamus and hypothalamus as the seat of emotional experience. These two small structures are located under the part of the brain cortex we think of as gray matter. The hypothalamus is a major endocrine (hormonal) regulatory center that influences emotional behavior; the thalamus links the cerebral or "thinking" part of your brain (speech, memory, and intelligence) to the rest of your body. When these glands act, the researchers theorized, all parts of the body, including the part of the brain that recognizes emotions, are aroused simultaneously. We see injustice, and then act and feel angry at the same time. But what is the link between the thalamus and the hypothalamus?

By the thirties, researchers had an answer: the limbic system. The limbic system is a loose network of lower-brain structures and nerve pathways that includes the hypothalamus, which in turn modulates our heart rate, blood pressure, muscle tension, sweating, and respiration. The conclusion, therefore, was that the hypothalamus controls our bodies' expressions of emotions, but it is the limbic system that perceives them and carries them to other parts of the brain, where they become our thoughts. Today this is still our working model for the mind/body connection.

In 1954, we learned more when James Olds implanted electrodes in the hypothalamuses of rats. The rats enjoyed the stimulation from the electrode so much that they learned to press a bar to activate it. In fact, the rats pressed the bar thousands of times to get the pleasurable stimulation, until they dropped of exhaustion and starvation. This is how the portion of the hypothalamus where the electrodes were placed came to be known as the pleasure center of the brain. Humans having brain surgery say they too find that stimulation of parts of the hypothalamus can be pleasurable. But stimulation of other parts of the hypothalamus produces rage. We now know the hypothalamus to be the center for sexual arousal, hunger, sleep, and body temperature, also.

Soon after the hypothalamus gets the message that an emotion is in motion, it sends a signal to the pituitary gland and then to other glands to release hormones. These powerful chemical substances flood the body, producing the familiar physical sensations of emotion. One of the most important of the hormones is adrenaline, likely to surge whenever we are threatened or angry. This and other hormones travel through our bloodstream to our muscles, heart, lungs, intestines, sweat glands, blood vessels, liver, and kidneys, where they prepare us physically to meet an emergency. This reaction to adrenaline is called the "flight or fight reaction" and it can make us feel fearful or angry long after the original cause is gone.

More current research tells us that other biochemicals that seem to influence mood are endorphins, the body's natural painkillers. Researchers suspect that endorphins rule the feelings of well-being that emanate from a good run to a good cry. Endorphins are also called opioids because they stimulate the same brain structures that heroin and other opium derivatives do, and produce the same euphoria. Endorphins must connect with target cells in the brain called opiate receptors to do their work. The endorphins fit into the receptors the way a key fits into a lock.

When researchers blocked the opiate receptors, they learned much about the power of endorphins. In one very fascinating experiment, Avram Goldstein, of Stanford University, gathered a group of volunteers who enjoyed music so much it sent ecstatic shivers up and down their spine. After the listeners had been given opiate blockers, they reported feeling far less rapture upon hearing their preferred music—a demonstration, the researchers believe, that endorphins play a role in this type of pleasure.

Emotion's Expressions

Current research also teaches us about the role of the brain's cortex in our expression of emotions.

You have probably heard about the brain's two halves—scientists call them the left and right hemispheres. Although the hemispheres are connected by the corpus callosum, each seems to have its specialties. The left hemisphere, in general, controls language, labels, and logic. (You can remember which is which by linking the "l's" in *left* with the "l's" in *language, labels, and logic.* The right hemisphere is more involved in visual-spatial functions and three aspects of emotion:

1. the perception and recognition of others' emotions based on their facial expressions and their voice tones
2. the interpretation of the emotional significance of situations
3. the organization of patterns of emotional reactions

When the right hemisphere is damaged, patients will often act indifferent to a disorder or a disaster. It's as if the left hemisphere *knows* but just doesn't seem to *care*, according to psychologist Neil

Carlson of the University of Massachusetts. When two Yale University researchers, Geoffrey Ahern and Gary Schwartz, measured electrical activity in the brains of thirty-three healthy college students, they picked up more activity in the right hemisphere than in the left when they created negative emotions in their experimental subjects. A Yale graduate student, Carrie Schaffer, and colleagues at the State University of New York at Purchase found more right-hemisphere activity in depressed students than in students who were not depressed. In people with brain injuries, the closer the injury is to the front of the right hemisphere, the more likely it is to affect the expression of emotions but not the recognition of others' emotions, says neuropsychiatrist Robert Robinson, of the Johns Hopkins School of Medicine. According to neurologist E. D. Ross, damage to the back of the right hemisphere affects recognition but not emotional expression.

Neuropsychologist Don Tucker, of the University of Oregon, says that *either* hemisphere can experience emotions, but that each half has its characteristic style of experience. The left hemisphere is alert: Both happy expectation and nervous anxiety are possible there. The right hemisphere is sensuous and restful. For example, awareness, which we would normally place in the left brain, would in the right brain be a calm awareness. Are you "left-brained" or "right-brained"? How about your child?

Wherever the seat of emotions lies in the brain, many of its outward aspects are the same around the world because emotional expressions, especially the ones that appear on our faces, are usually basic. We do not have to learn them. People who have been deaf and blind since birth can cry, laugh, and frown. If a stranger who does not speak your language approaches you, you will still be able to tell whether many expressions are pleasant or unpleasant, accepting or rejecting, certain or uncertain. The startled look is also fairly universal—the eyes close and the mouth widens as it would in a grin. Of course, there are just enough cultural variations on facial expressions to keep life interesting. While Americans usually raise their eyebrows and widen their eyes to show surprise, a Chinese person with widened eyes may be angry, and a Japanese person may show regret by a smile.

But the greatest differences in emotions and emotional expression is not between different cultures—it is between the different sexes. Let's now look at the "opposite sex" from a passions point of view.

His and Hers

Vive la différence! Long live the difference, as the French are fond of saying.

Of course, women and men have similarities. We both can be tough and we both can be gentle. We both deserve to be listened to, cared about, and treated with respect.

But men and women can also differ quite dramatically in their emotional experiences. The following accounts are from universities and research institutions around the world.

Girls and Women

- Girls age six to eleven report more sad events than boys the same age.
- Women who looked at photographs of faces could recognize sadness more accurately than men.
- Girls are more likely to blame themselves rather than others for problems.
- High school girls report more depression than boys.
- Ninth-grade girls have greater fear of death, insects, injury, and being alone. Rather than confronting their fears, they are more likely to escape to the protection and companionship of other people.
- Anorexia nervosa, a serious eating disorder, is a far more common stress reaction in girls than boys.
- Women have a two-to-one greater incidence of depression than men.
- Women report more anxiety than men.

- College women are more jealous than college men over situations in which a lover spends time on a hobby or with family members.
- Jealousy in marriage is correlated with self-reports of low self-esteem for women but not for men.
- Women have more friends than men and rely more on these friends for emotional support and conversations about feelings.

As we can see, a quick summary of research reveals that more females than males experience the emotions of sadness, depression, anxiety, jealousy, and sadness. They also report more self-blame, eating disorders, self-examination, and—happily—supportive friendships. Compare all this to males.

Boys and Men

- In high school students, anger is more commonly reported in boys than girls.
- Men who looked at photographs of faces were better than women at recognizing anger.
- Boys are more likely to look outside themselves for explanations of problems.
- Boys age nine rate themselves "less afraid" than girls. Both boys and girls say that "other boys" are less fearful than "other girls."
- Ninth-grade boys say they fear animals and heights; they are more likely than girls to cope with fear by attacking the source of a problem.
- Boys are about three times more prone to hyperactivity, with its mood swings, frustration, and sudden rages, than girls.
- Men are more likely to deal with depression by trying to distract themselves.

A summary of male behavior includes scapegoating, attacking, and destroying, problems like hyperactivity and distractibility, and the reports of the emotion called anger.

My Passions Survey findings support the idea that, whether by nature or nurture, men's and women's emotional profiles can be quite different.

Emotions in Disguise

Although we all probably have the capacity for experiencing all emotions, many of us report a limited repertoire. Sometimes this means we haven't needed or exercised a particular emotion. But sometimes when we say we never feel certain emotions, we are feeling them and pretending we don't. The human mind is not naturally deceptive, but what it often does is find ways to avoid pain. If a piece of reality is causing us great stress or conflict, we may give up that piece of reality in order to protect or defend ourselves against the conflict. This is what we are doing when we "don't see" the telltale signs of drug abuse in our children or we "ignore" the clues that our husband is having an affair. It is called denial. Men and women both use this defense mechanism, but for quite different reasons.

Some women said they never feel:	Some men said they never feel:
1. rage	1. infatuation
2. despair	2. contentment
3. infatuation	3. despair

The Emotions Women Never Feel: Rage, Despair, Infatuation

The one emotion that the largest number of women say they never feel is rage. We do feel anger—no one denied that! Enraged rarely, angered frequently—if you look at women's passions as a continuum, we are aware of the precursor, anger, but not the fully developed peak emotion, rage.

This is probably because, traditionally, rage has not been a feminine emotion. A society that valued lace, lipstick, and lullabies was not likely to place much value on a woman who hurled angry words or dinner plates. In the past, strong women often found themselves alone. Some of us learned to avoid or overlook situations that would have enraged us in a better world. A married woman with no financial assets of her own and two children she loves may not "choose" to see her husband flirting with her friend. Our defense mechanism mobilizes us to reduce potential conflict between unacceptable angry impulses and our idealized view of ourself or another. We literally block out a part of reality in order not to deal with conflict. Sometimes we even develop symptoms to bolster our denial and make it easier for ourselves to avoid a conflict. A woman who gave up her job as a travel writer to be at home with children may develop a fear of flying. A well-educated woman whose husband is extremely jealous and possessive may suddenly find herself in the grip of agoraphobia, a fear of going outside. A career woman who hits the glass ceiling—the limit to which the men in her company will allow women to rise—might convince herself that it makes sense for women to choose not to climb the corporate ladder. All of these women have avoided a conflict about their rage.

By hiding our rage, we also avoid enraging others. Rage often begets rage, which can then mean a threat or reality of physical violence—since most men are physically larger and stronger than most women. A woman's rage can engender a brush-off instead—and once he slams out of the house, she has more to be angry about. Her rage can even provoke a sexual invitation: "You're so cute when you're angry," the leading man says to the fuming woman before he takes her in his arms and tries to make her forget why she was so mad. Now she's really enraged! But it's not a woman's fear of others' reactions to her rage that is the primary motivation for her denial. It is usually her fear that her rage will hurt others. It is incompatible with the nurturing role many women treasure. But what of the boss who does not give credit; the man who is a little too rough in bed; the friend who betrays; the pain, the obstacles, the losses . . . when can we no longer close our eyes? We can seem serene or accepting (even to ourselves), but rage often lies not far beneath these states of grace.

Women may also be legitimately better at dealing with potentially enraging situations. By our natures, we may be more apt to use words to defuse a situation before it explodes into physical action. Certainly, we have the capacity to be enraged, but we do not use it as often as men do. The female's threshold for putting anger into action seems to be much higher then the male's threshold—it takes longer to be reached. Common situations like being cut off in traffic or cut out of an assignment may anger us, but do not usually enrage us. It may take something as dramatic as a personal attack to activate our rage.

Nearly as many women as men said they do not feel despair, either. Despair has to do with giving up, with a sense of helplessness. Despair suggests that we can do nothing about our fate. Although women have a much higher risk of depression than men, it is good that women feel as little of despair as men do.

Although TV, romance novels, and magazine fiction make it seem that no woman can survive unless she is head-over-heels in love, 20 percent of respondents say they never feel infatuated. Men accuse women of being too susceptible to romantic notions, but in my survey, 55 percent of women said *men* were more easily infatuated! In fact, most research tells us that men, not women, are more apt to fall in love first, leave love last, suffer more during breakups, and more frequently marry for "love," perhaps because they can afford to. Women seem to enjoy romance and sexual attraction—but as recreational reading, television viewing, or temporary distractions. The woman of the nineties is very practical.

The Emotions Men Never Feel:
Infatuation, Contentment, Despair

More than a quarter (27 percent) of men in my survey said that though they can feel love, they never feel infatuation. Is it the economy? Are these men too busy working? Is it fear of feelings? Or fear of intimacy? Infatuation is a real letting go, a release of control, and perhaps this is very difficult for many men. Even in questionnaires where they are guaranteed anonymity, men may be reluctant to admit to being out of control.

It may also be that some men, like women, have learned to recognize sexual attraction as just that. Maybe the answer would have been different if we asked: "Have you ever been carried away by sexual attraction?" Or, "Have you ever been swept away by romance?" Remember, other surveys tell us that men marry for love more often than women, and men hang on to dying relationships longer than women also. And this survey tells us that ¼ of men said they had indeed felt the peaks of infatuation.

Just short of 23 percent of men also said they do not feel contentment. This is sad; it shows to what extent some men are measuring themselves and how acutely they are feeling failure. These men are not allowing themselves to sit back and appreciate themselves, their lives, their blessings. Overall, a large percentage of men said they never feel positive emotions, infatuation (27 percent) and contentment (23 percent), while many women say they never feel negative emotions (rage, 22.2 percent; despair, 20 percent).

Often-Felt Emotions

Men and women also differ when it comes to the emotion they feel most often. Though we both feel the same three emotions most frequently, their order is telling. Women emphasize the negative, men, the positive.

Women most often feel:
1. anxiety
2. contentment
3. hope

Men most often feel:
1. contentment
2. hope
3. anxiety

Anxiety   Anxiety, a negative emotion, heads the women's most-often-felt list. Only half as many men say it is their most frequent emotion. Why more women than men? It is tempting to say that men are causing women to be anxious, and in one way that is true. In my survey, women often named fathers and husbands as two of their greatest sources of anxiety, because these are the people from whom women want to hide their negative feelings. Men, on the other hand, rarely mentioned people of either sex as causes of anxiety. Both women and men mentioned performance anxiety—on tests, in life in general—as well.

Contentment   Only about a fifth of women say contentment is their most often felt emotion. What a shame! We have worked so hard to earn respect at work and consideration at home. Many of us are successful in our careers, own our own homes or apartments, make enough money to buy ourselves the things we want, but we feel it is not enough. Although we have further to go—women are still not paid as much as men for the same work—we can certainly afford to look around and feel some satisfaction with the distance we have come. Perhaps it is time to break the habit of dissatisfaction while continuing to make progress working toward equality.

Although more than one in three men say contentment is their most common emotion, *one fifth of men never feel it*! Men, apparently, vary enormously. It is reassuring, at least, that so many men are finding their lives satisfactory and enjoying the feeling, but both sexes have far to go toward experiencing more contentment.

Hope   The human mind has the capacity to understand the concept of future, and this future we imagine for ourselves is often more bright and beautiful than the time we live in now. This trait has probably helped us survive. Certainly, it has made many gray todays more bearable. It is wonderful to see it in the top three emotions that both men and women feel.

But the men in the study were nearly twice as hopeful as women. Perhaps because men often feel they have more control over their world than do women. They may dare to hope because they know they have more power, time, and money to make their hope real. On the other hand, although some men say they hold the faithful hope of belief in God, this is true for even more females than males.

Overall, in this survey women denied feeling negative emotions and reported that they did feel anxiety most frequently; men admitted to negative emotions and felt contentment and hope the most frequently. Could it be that accepting and expressing negative emotions permits you to be more in touch with all your emotions—the positive ones also? Possibly. Many psychologists would agree.

Could it mean that women really do lead more anxiety-provoking lives than men do? This is also possible. The women of the nineties are still piling on roles, are we not? We are still catching up with men financially; we are waiting longer to start families. Could it be that the quality of life really is better for men or that their needs are simpler or more simply met? Perhaps it means all of this, with some physical predisposition thrown in.

Could it also mean that when it comes to answering survey questions, men do not recognize or report their emotions as accurately and honestly as women? Certainly possible. Men may feel that reporting anxiety, even on a questionnaire, shows weakness.

Our Favorite Emotions

Men and women have another difference as well: Women value love, but men, given the choice, prefer joy.

Women's favorite emotion:	Men's favorite emotion:
1. love (32 percent)	1. joy (42 percent)
2. joy (31 percent)	2. love (32 percent)
3. contentment (27 percent)	3. contentment (13 percent)
4. hope (8 percent)	4. hope (10 percent)
5. courage (2 percent)	5. courage (3 percent)

Here seems to be more evidence that men of today are self-oriented and women are people-oriented. By naming love as their favorite emotion, women are confirming how important other people are. Women love love. Joy, on the other hand, can take many forms— some that need other people and some that do not.

How Society Shapes Our Emotions

Why do men and women feel and express emotions differently? One reason may be that our mothers, fathers, and our society "expect" us to be very different and then treat us as if we are very different. Two researchers, J. Meyer and B. Sobieszek, for example, showed many fathers videotapes of seventeen-month-old children. When the men were told that the child they were looking at was a boy, they described the child as active, alert, and aggressive. When fathers who saw the SAME CHILD were told it was a girl, they described it as cuddly, passive, and delicate. Other studies tell us that fathers, mothers, nurses, and teachers treat males and females differently from the day they are born. If this seems sexist, remember that the fathers learned these stereotypes from their own mothers as well as their fathers. We inherit from our parents not only a set of genes but a set of attitudes. The way our parents see us shapes they way we see ourselves.

Society also shapes men and women through reinforcement. Women, for example, *learn* to use their ability to reach out for other people, and each time we do, the people around us approve and thus reinforce our action. Men, on the other hand, usually learn to use their capacity for independence to handle things without help from outside. Men in our society learn to endure physical pain, denying themselves the right to recognize a physical feeling and ask for relief. Though men usually have more physical strength than women, it is women who, with society's blessing, follow up on physical pain by seeing a doctor. This may be one reason that the average American woman lives more than seven years longer than her male counterpart. The modes of behavior we learn may cost many men their lives.

The Physical Differences

Physiology may also have something to do with the reasons women and men differ emotionally.

Scientists have come across some interesting differences between the male and female brains. For one, the *corpus callosum*, the band of fibers that connects the left half of the brain to the right half, seems to be more innervated in women than in men. They are still not sure exactly what this finding means, but some researchers guess that it may indicate a stronger connection between the parts of the brain that have to do with speech. As you may know, girls usually start talking sooner than boys, and women have traditionally been more verbal than men. It may also indicate, according to some, a tendency to use *both* hemispheres rather than to specialize. This would mean that females would more often combine the logic of the left brain with the visual/spatial abilities of the right: balancing the checkbook and decorating the house. We can "do it all." We are good at it all. Thus we are more likely to be trying to "do it all."

We also know that males have higher levels of some hormones and females have higher levels of others. Testosterone, for example, is known as the male hormone and estrogen as the female hormone, although men and women have levels of each. Testosterone has been called the aggression hormone. One study of college wrestlers turned up higher testosterone levels in winners than in losers! Another study found that aggressive hockey players had more testosterone than their more easygoing teammates. And a third study concludes that aggressive prisoners had almost double the testosterone level of the average male not in prison.

Testosterone also correlates with other types of aggressive behavior. Penn State researchers found a high level of the male hormone androstenedione in boys who lied, were disobedient, and did poorly in school. In girls, androstenedione correlated with defiance, dominating behavior, anger toward parents, and concentration problems.

It is unlikely that hormones alone dictate our emotional profiles, but they may, instead, set our *thresholds* for emotional reactions— perhaps our readiness for certain emotional responses. Will research in the nineties find that "male hormones" lower the threshold for assertive reactions to the environment and that "female hormones" prime our readiness to react verbally? We will find out.

Is the Gender Gap Closing?

It seems that the gender gap is narrowing a bit. Society now encourages girls to try traditional boys' activities (girls can play "boys' sports"), and boys dabble in what has always been thought of as girls' work (baby-sitting and cooking, for example). The SATs

(Scholastic Aptitude Test) may tell us about some effects of society's changes. In 1947, girls scored higher than boys in spelling, language, clerical speed and accuracy, and verbal ability. The boys outpaced the girls in mechanical, verbal, and abstract reasoning, space relations, and numerical ability. By 1980, the only difference remaining was the gap in math performance in the later years of high school.

The separation between women's work and men's is narrowing, too. We have more job options than ever before: Women are now firefighters, telephone-repair people, and police officers. More than half of all women now work outside the home. We have more reasons to work. We need the money and working has been found to increase self-esteem and reduce the risk of depression in women. We have more encouragement to work. Feminism supported women's forays into the world. And while women flexed their career muscles, many men took the opportunity to flex their emotions: They learned to look inward.

Finally, many parents are trying to equalize the approval and reinforcement mechanism that shapes male and female roles. We have all become experts in sexism and are more careful not to crush sensitivity in boys or courage in girls. Today's parents have the confidence to buy their little boy the stuffed animal he asks for and let the little girl choose the boy's-style jeans over the frilly pink things. It is a society-wide experiment, and in five or ten years its effects should begin to show in the emotional makeup of the men and women these children become.

I look forward to then surveying emotions again. We may find that some of the gaps between our emotional experiences have grown smaller. And the ones that remain? Some may be everlasting differences between men and women. Others may not.

MANAGING YOUR NEGATIVE PASSIONS

Most of us think of passions as positive emotions. To most of us, the prime passion means the most intense kind of love, that magnificent physical, emotional, spiritual union of two people. We dream of it, we worship it, and when it arrives we indulge it. We feel that the passion is bigger than we are, so we give up our control and ride the wave. Passion is an emotion we seek, and we often stretch the definition of passion to mean an intense feeling for anything: art, good food, a political idea, fine wine, jewelry, a charity, a sport, a collection.

Passion can also seem like something we would rather not meet on a dark street, something out of a hidden box of hideous gargoyles. We can dislike someone or something "with a passion," and we can plunge as deeply into seas of sadness, regret, or alarm as we can into love and flounder there without a direction. If love is a passion, so are rage, fear, despair, and guilt. They are just as physical and just as emotional.

We dread our negative passions—and we love to talk about them after they have passed. One California researcher decided to find out what emotions we like to discuss most, so with permission from his subjects he taped twenty-six of their phone conversations randomly. Every speaker mentioned more negative emotions than positive ones. Maybe you do that yourself—you find it easier to talk about your downs than your ups. What story do you save to tell your best friend: the one about the overwhelming love you felt for your boyfriend last night or the detail-by-detail account of the knock-down, drag-out fight you had with your boss? Most of us would tell the fight story, and with some sort of pleasure.

It is human nature to savor the dramatic. We elicit sympathy and support from others by telling the tales of our troubles. The retelling also helps to desensitize us to our past and future terrors. Have you heard of a support group for joyous, hopeful, smitten, or awed people? It is quite likely that we are still recounting the same stories years after our anxieties have subsided and feelings have faded, because we find negative emotions more intense than positive ones. Just compare the intensity ratings of the positive and negative emotions in the Passions Survey.

EMOTIONS WE FIND MOST INTENSE

%	Anger	Anxiety	Rage	Guilt	Fear	Despair	Jealousy	Love	Joy	Hope	Infatuation
22.1	X										
20.8	X										
19.5	X										
18.2	X							X			
16.9	X	X						X			
15.6	X	X						X			
14.3	X	X						X			
13.0	X	X						X			
11.7	X	X						X			
10.4	X	X						X			
9.1	X	X						X			
7.8	X	X	X					X	X		
6.5	X	X	X	X	X			X	X	X	
5.2	X	X	X	X	X	X		X	X	X	
3.9	X	X	X	X	X	X		X	X	X	
2.6	X	X	X	X	X	X		X	X	X	
1.3	X	X	X	X	X	X	X	X	X	X	X

| Negative Emotions | Positive Emotions |

Why do we find negative emotions more intense? Maybe because they overtake us against our will. Instead of feeling uplifted, we feel downtrodden. We feel every tug that pulls us down, and most of us fight the entire way. When those negative emotions end, the feeling of release is intense.

We not only tell our own tales of fear, guilt, rage, and despair, but we like to listen other people's stories as well. Hearing of others' fear, rage, despair, and guilt sometimes make us feel better. *It happened to her, not to me, so I'm safe for now,* we think. Why do newspapers that chronicle the day's violence and pain sell in such volume? Why are we drawn to confession phone-ins and soap operas? Probably because we need to feel that once again, we have escaped the evil eye.

As much as we may be drawn to tales of woe, we also find that negative emotions make us more uncomfortable than positive emotions. Heading the list of emotions that feel most unpleasant to us are anxiety, guilt, and fear.

EMOTIONS WE FIND MOST UNCOMFORTABLE

	Anxiety	Guilt	Fear	Despair	Rage	Anger	Jealousy	Infatuation	Joy	Contentment	Love
18.0	x										
16.8	x	x	x								
15.6	x	x	x								
14.4	x	x	x	x							
13.2	x	x	x	x	x						
12.0	x	x	x	x	x						
10.8	x	x	x	x	x						
9.6	x	x	x	x	x	x					
8.4	x	x	x	x	x	x					
7.2	x	x	x	x	x	x	x				
6.0	x	x	x	x	x	x	x				
4.8	x	x	x	x	x	x	x				
3.6	x	x	x	x	x	x	x				
2.4	x	x	x	x	x	x	x				
1.2	x	x	x	x	x	x	x	x	x	x	x
%	Anxiety	Guilt	Fear	Despair	Rage	Anger	Jealousy	Infatuation	Joy	Contentment	Love

| Negative Emotions | Positive Emotions |

Luck and life create highs for us (love, joy, hope, and awe, among them), and we can learn to prolong these and create more. But luck and life also offer us lows (fear, rage, despair, guilt, and many more). Sometimes we can learn how to avoid them. Sometimes there is no escape. That's the bad news. The good news, though, is that negative passions are often signs of conflict, and conflict can be part of growth and change. We need to get comfortable with the phenomenon of negative passion.

Normal or Not?

It came over you like a thunder cloud: One minute you were fine, the next you were in a storm, helpless and spinning with bad feelings. After it was over, you could still feel the effects of the hormones and tensions that took over your body. What happened?

Something that may be very normal.

Fear, rage, despair, guilt, and many more negative passions are often quite appropriate to many situations:

Your husband has an affair, you find out about it, and you feel enraged. That is appropriate rage.

Your toddler spills his milk for the third time that day; you slap his hand hard in frustration and then feel guilty. That is appropriate guilt.

You are anxious because tomorrow you will go before a panel of faculty members to defend your doctoral dissertation. Perfectly appropriate anxiety.

You are out for a walk when you see running toward you a pit bull that has escaped from its pen. Appropriate fear.

Your father is terminally ill; the despair you feel is appropriate.

As much as we dislike feeling negative passions, they can lead us to action. The despairing daughter will be forced to reduce outside commitments and conserve her energy to help take care of her sick father. Perhaps this concentration of effort will allow her the energy to call one more doctor, who will be the one who can help her understand her father's diagnosis. The rage of the woman whose husband has cheated on her propels her to call her therapist for help—and a lawyer, too. In her guilt, the toddler's mother vows never to slap him again for such a small, age-appropriate accident. The doctoral candidate decides to channel her nervous energy into an extra few hours of preparation until she feels more confident. The walker who encounters the ferocious dog takes advantage of fear's shot of adrenaline by jumping a fence *fast.*

Get Rid of Inappropriate Reactions

Not all negative emotions are appropriate or useful, of course. You can spare yourself much suffering in the future by making sure that your emotional reactions are both. An inappropriate emotion is something like a check you write out and then send to the wrong address: You feel that you paid, but the account stays open. Inappropriate emotion is a waste of your energy that can do no good and may even do harm.

The Practice Effect   One explanation for inappropriate emotions is the practice effect. The more you have experienced an emotion in the past, the easier it is to call it out in the present, even when it is not called for. Fear, guilt, despair, and rage all become easier, too easy, with practice.

> Jake is an angry man. No matter what you say or do, he finds a way to take it personally and so is angry about it. If you suggest an easier way for him to slice the turkey, he takes it as a personal criticism and stalks out of the room. If at the dinner table two people talk for more than a few minutes without including him, he accuses them of shutting him out. If the photo developer loses his negatives, Jake smolders for two days. At the office, he rages

about being excluded from the flow of information, which quite likely is true, since he always finds something to be angry about, which obstructs other people's progress.

Jake has made a habit of anger. In fact, when he feels a good mood coming on, he becomes very uncomfortable.

I can tell you something about Jake that may help you understand his anger. He lost his father when he was seven, and his mother felt angry about it. His mother in turn displaced her anger to Jake. Then his mother fell sick and Jake became angry. The young boy learned to give anger as well as receive it. To him, anger was synonymous with his mother, home, and childhood. By now he has a very low threshold for anger. As many people do, he prolongs his physical and emotional anger even after the source of it is gone by going over and over in his mind the last situation that upset him.

I am not making excuses, however, for people who have made *habits* of negative emotions. Our emotional scripts today may have been written in our childhood, but as adults we can stop rehearsing these scripts, analyze our behavior, and start managing our negative emotions. And we can start today.

Displaced Emotions   Another reason for inappropriate emotion is *displacement*, the misdirection of an appropriate reaction to an inappropriate target.

It is 7:05 in the morning and Marcia's husband, John, wants to be on the 7:26 train. At this moment he is making an issue over the fact that Marcia has not sorted his socks. Helpfully, Marcia finds John two socks that match and shows him her best understanding smile as she hands them to him, but he does not notice. Then he goes off to work.

Marcia is left alone with McTavish, her little Scottie dog, who has tracked mud onto the foyer carpet. She growls a command to McTavish, opens the door and ushers the dog out roughly by the collar, fuming about the extra work the dog has caused her.

Marcia has displaced her annoyance to poor McTavish. The emotion is legitimate, but it is inappropriately placed. The emotion (annoyance) didn't connect with its source (John, the husband). It's therefore likely that the same situation will happen again, because Marcia has done nothing to recognize or address it. Meanwhile, the innocent McTavish will do his best to stay out of the way when Marcia has her fits of pique.

Family pets are not the only unfortunate receptors for displaced emotions. Children, the elderly, *anyone* who happens to be weak or in the way can bear the brunt of a displaced emotion. People have long memories and carry scars—if you are misdirecting emotion to an innocent target, do the kind thing and put the emotion back in its place.

Society hands us a lot of emotions to displace. The traffic is frustrating. The evening news is mostly bad, and it makes us mad or sad. The magazines we read are full of alarming articles. The economy seems to be on the skids, and we are scared. However tempting it may be to take it out on the people around the dinner table, it is important to keep negative emotions that begin outside from entering our interactions with loved ones inside.

Families under financial or health stresses need to be especially careful, because the source of the stress (a problem at home) and a convenient place to displace it (loved ones) are very close together. When a child dies, there is a higher chance that the parents' marriage will break up rather than become more bonded, because the parents displace their pain onto each other. Each parent looks at the spouse, sees the child, and feels the loss again and again.

Anticipatory Emotion   Anticipatory emotion is a special breed of emotion that exists in the present as a reaction to something in the future. You have probably experienced it yourself. If you have ever imagined the worst that could occur and then worked yourself into a lather about it, only to find that nothing of the kind ended up happening, you have lived an anticipatory emotion.

We are all prone to anticipatory emotion. Mothers are especially proficient at anticipatory anxiety and fear: We imagine our children being abducted, hit by cars, disliked by teachers, rejected by peers, seduced by drugs, making bad marriages. We lose a lot of sleep over these eventualities. In reality, most of the time they never come to pass. This kind of anticipatory anxiety and fear is inappropriate but hard to dislodge. Rage and despair are equally tough to move. (Guilt, it is interesting to note, is rarely anticipated.)

To rid yourself of anticipatory emotion, try to separate fact from fiction. What is worth worrying about? What is not? Think about the past: How much energy have you wasted on anticipatory emotion? What unlikely situations do you anticipate most often? The key to calm is within your own heart and mind.

Anticipatory emotions can be appropriate too, sometimes even useful. They can be based on sensitivity to subtle cues and lightning-fast subliminal information-processing. If you find yourself worrying that your lover is having an affair, for example, ask yourself if you have picked up information that suggests there is a *basis* for your concern. Has his behavior been slightly different? Is there something about his situation that has left him vulnerable to temptation? Have you noticed a subtle change in his appearance, his schedule, or his treatment of you? If your answers are yes, then your anticipatory anxiety may serve you well and you can perhaps now address the facts. But if your answers are no time and time again, you must remember this exercise when you begin to ruminate about any dire possibility. To separate fact from fiction, bring yourself back to the present. Look around you at immediate reality. Give yourself a *real* project or problem to dwell on. And cultivate an attitude of resigned acceptance toward unknowable future catastrophes. Don't waste one drop of adrenaline that won't be used.

If the future event that worries you is assured, however, handle the pre-event anxiety by using the extra adrenaline to do whatever you can to prepare for the situation. Suppose you are suffering from a bad case of nerves over an upcoming stage performance. The show is sold out, and barring a fire in the theater or a serious illness on your part (you would be happy with either), you will be on stage tomorrow night at 8 P.M. in front of an expectant audience. You could count yourself lucky for feeling shaky now. You could channel your energy into a review of your lines, or you could walk your stage pattern. If the theater were open, you could even take your butterflies onto the stage with you, play to the empty seats, and take command of the theater. By curtain time, you would be excellently prepared and perhaps feel more in control than if you had not had anticipatory anxiety to channel.

Change Your Choices

You have now winnowed out the practice effect, displaced emotion, and unnecessary anticipatory emotion. What else can you do to reduce the number of negative emotions in the future?

You can change the way you handle choices. Sometimes this can be very simple. Plane rides scare you? For short trips, give yourself a choice: Drive, take the train, or board a ship. For long trips, give yourself no choice. Make the decision to fly and then do not change or review the decision again. Your approach to your fears and anxieties should be passive acceptance of them all: "If I crash, I crash," or, "If I feel trapped, I'll survive the feeling." Treat your ambivalence as an inconvenience, not a dire warning. Save yourself from the torture of making the choice and unmaking it again and again.

I realize that putting distance between yourself and the source of negative emotions is not always so simple. Say you have chosen a career in which very few jobs are available and the search for work leaves you in despair at the end of each day. A career change may be the right thing. But the courses necessary to enter a new field cost money, and you may be starting at the bottom of the ladder again. Prepare yourself to pay this price for what you want. The same goes for the woman who lives in constant fear because her husband hits her: She does not want to stay within the reach of his arm, but finding a new place to live where he cannot find her and then actually leaving—knowing that if he catches up with her, he will hit her even harder—takes more courage and resources than many women think they have. Anyone who needs help managing a negative emotion can usually find low-cost help—at churches, in free clinics, even with individual psychologists, social workers, psychiatric nurses, and psychiatrists, who are often willing to accept what a client can pay. Or call teaching hospitals, women's centers, state or county chapters of the American Psychological Association and American Psychiatric Association to get references for licensed, qualified help (see Appendix).

Change Your Reactions

Another way to reduce the amount of negative emotion in your life is to adjust the way you process your emotions. If you find your threshold for negative reactions is too low, you can try counter-conditioning. For example: Your child frequently does not pick up her toys, your husband does not clean up his workshop, or your roommate leaves the kitchen a mess every time she cooks a meal. You are annoyed, bordering on furious. First, get yourself totally relaxed. It is impossible to experience two physical states at the same time, and fury is about as different from relaxation as can be. Take some deep breaths and relax every muscle in your body. Now imagine that the person has left just a small mess—a child has left one piece of a puzzle on the floor, for example. Picture yourself calmly picking it up and putting it away without losing self-control. You are learning a new reaction to an old stimulus. A behavior that you practice becomes more and more comfortable, and you are more likely to repeat it. This puts the practice effect to excellent use.

Now, remaining relaxed, imagine that first the one piece and then one more is on the floor. Then, starting from the beginning *each* time, see if you can stay relaxed as you picture two pieces, then three, then five, and then the whole puzzle. Keep practicing until you can see this in your mind and remain relaxed. You have brought the exercise to a successful end when you can envision the child getting up and leaving a terrible mess on the floor and adrenaline does not flood through you. Now you are ready to graduate: Try relaxing in front of a *real* mess rather than an imaginary one. This exercise uses progressive desensitization; you start with the situation that calls forth your negative emotion and break it into a hierarchy of manageable fragments. You start with the smallest, simplest, manageable fraction and build tolerance from there. Once you can confront the situation without automatic negative reactions, you can make real choices about how you want to manage the situation.

Instead of starting with the most manageable item on your emotional agenda, some psychotherapists may help you confront the least manageable one. This technique is called flooding. Flooding is sometimes used for people who are phobic. Suppose you have a phobia of snakes. In the progressive desensitization we just discussed, you might start with a picture and then go to a plastic worm; in flooding, you might be shown a whole cage of boa constrictors or hold one in your hand until your emotional response is exhausted and you see that you can survive your fear. It seems that the less you act on the fight-or-flight response, the less adrenaline pours out in the same situation the next time. Although flooding can be useful, Dr. Gordon Ball, associate professor of psychiatry at the New York State Psychiatric Institute, calls it "a miserable therapy," because patients must suffer through their worst anxieties before they get better. If you feel that you'd like to try it, know that it really belongs in a therapist's office—this powerful therapy is not to be tried alone.

Another way to change your appraisal and arousal level is to change your thinking. Approaches that rely on thought are called cognitive techniques, because another word for thinking is *cognition*. According to cognitive therapist Dr. Albert Ellis, founder of the Institute for Rational Emotive Therapy in New York, the following are some common triggers of emotional discomfort:

> failure or rejection;
> mistreatment at the hands of other people;
> demands that are hard, unpleasant, or painful.

To alter your sensitivity to these and other triggers, Ellis suggests changing the way you see these triggers—that is, changing your cognitions. Remember chronically angry Jake? Let us say his anger is directed at others because he wants to mistreat before he is mistreated. If he realized that his anger was part of a strategy that was not working well, he could interrupt or neutralize his anger and choose a different strategy for avoiding mistreatment. He might also learn to perceive others' behavior as information about *them*, not as information about their feelings toward him! For example, he could choose to see an unanswered phone as a sign that a friend might be ill, busy, or upset, not as a sign of rejection. Jake may always react negatively to rejection, but he can learn to see fewer and fewer situations as rejection.

Besides helping you change the way you *see* a situation, thinking can help you change the way you *react* to it. Because altering your final action is a decision you have to make consciously, you cannot change your reactions while your brain is on automatic pilot. Here is an example:

> June, a secretary, was recently fired. She decided not to indulge her despair over her lost job but rather to go out for the evening and celebrate that she would not ever again have to hear her boss

call her "my gal." While she was out, she met someone interesting and got a lead on a new job.

Before she even left the house, June was already ahead: She knew that at the very least, someone would serve her dinner! Here is another story, about a young medical student I know who *decided* how to react to a negative situation:

> Mitch had wanted to be a doctor for as long as he could remember. Now, however, he was less sure: He was standing before a table, and a cadaver (a dead person) lay in front of him, waiting for his scalpel. Mitch knew that this was the way to learn about the human body. But he wanted to run. He wanted to hide. He wanted to throw up. But he also wanted to be a doctor. So Mitch decided to proceed in spite of a full complement of unpleasant physical feelings and thoughts. Soon he felt better. At the end of an hour, he was surprised to find he was quite fascinated by what he was doing.

Mitch used a cognitive strategy when he *decided* to stick with the dissection, a task that was hard, unpleasant, and painful for him. The feedback he gave his fight-and-flight response was that it was not needed. The "strategy" worked, and soon, the response weakened and faded. Mitch then felt in control, and so can you.

The Keys to Comfort

You have now tossed out your practiced, displaced, and anticipatory emotions; you have adjusted your appraisal and arousal reactions, and you have learned to take action. Does this mean you will never suffer a negative emotion or passion again for as long as you live?

That is not a promise anyone can make. The only people who are completely immune from them arc dead! But while some negative passions are inevitable, fear of them is not.

In the last section, we talked about changing our thinking to change a potential emotional reaction or action. Now let us talk about using cognition to diminish negative emotions after they arrive.

By monitoring what we are feeling, even if we feel that we are being swept away by the full force of a strong emotion, we can avoid some feelings of being out of control. When you feel a negative passion coming on, study it—become fascinated by it. Has your heart suddenly started to pound? Are you perspiring? Gather this information. This monitoring will give you some welcome distance from uncomfortable feelings without denying the feelings. I had no idea I was so angry about this, you might think. Or, I'm amazed at how afraid I feel of that snake. Or, This is very uncomfortable for me. Or, I really can cry. Or, I didn't know that an assault on my appearance could evoke such rage. Do not try to stop your passion's progress. If you try to stop it, you will only succeed in slowing down the whole process, and it will take longer to get through it.

Consider the man who must cross a high bridge to get to fertile land. He has to leave the barren side in order to survive. But this man is afraid of heights. He starts to cross because he knows he must, then pauses in the middle of the bridge to look down. There, in the middle, he is overcome with anxiety at his fear of heights. He knows he is losing control, so he runs back to the side that is familiar. The key word here is *back*. He soon feels less anxious, but he knows that he must move on to survive and so he again starts across the bridge. Though he knows he is afraid of heights, he does not resist pausing again in the middle of the bridge and looking down. He freezes again, runs back again, and must go through the terror still again . . . and again.

You and I know that to survive he must eventually cross the bridge, but how could he save himself from so many terrified crossings? One way he could do it is by looking at his emotions, "monitoring," while crossing the bridge—rather than stopping and looking down. If you want to try "monitoring," try this. As an emotion like fear overtakes you, do not stop your progress. Observe yourself in the throes of emotion and learn all you can about yourself. This way you will not only be able to move through an emotion to its end, but also to grow emotionally. Remember, emotional growth is a lifelong process, not for children only.

There is, however, one caution about the "thinking" approach: Don't confuse "thinking" yourself through an emotion with rationalizing yourself out of an emotion. If thinking gets in the way of feeling, that is sometimes an indication that you are uncomfortable with the feeling. You may feel, for example, *Who am I to force my anger on others*? Your upbringing may have made you feel guilty about negative emotions. Or perhaps the people around you make you feel your fear or anger or anxiety or despair are worthless. No law that says one person's emotions are worth more or less than someone else's. Anyone who has made you feel that your feelings are unimportant is playing psychological power games with you. You have a right to your emotions, both positive and negative.

The final key to comfort is talking. Whenever we feel mystified or overwhelmed by our negative feelings, talking about them can help us sort things out and feel less isolated. We do not necessarily have to locate a professional listener or guidance counselor—a psychiatrist, psychologist, social worker, or psychiatric nurse. Talking to yourself on paper or even to the cat may be enough to help you hear yourself and crystallize your thoughts and *decide* if you need to take action. If you have the luxury of talking with a wise or sympathetic friend, you will learn even more about yourself.

Hidden Emotions, Hidden Sources

Sometimes we feel anxiety, rage, despair, guilt, or other negative passions and have no idea why. Perhaps we may wish to avoid confronting the source of the emotion: insecurity, illness, a specific guilt, marital problems, feelings of hatred, unbearable memories.

Or we may have buried anxiety, rage, despair, or guilt because they were confusing or inconvenient. Sometimes seemingly sourceless negative emotions can stem from biochemical imbalances such as PMS or paramenopausal changes, clinical depression, chronic illness, drug or medication use, abuse or withdrawal or alcohol abuse.

To get at the source of negative emotions, Sigmund Freud asked patients about their dreams. Freud believed that every object, action, and setting that appeared in a dream had significance. In the last few years, the pendulum has swung so far in the other direction that some researchers say that dreams are no more than a few random signals from your brain cells, left over from the day's thinking. Between the extreme symbolism of Freud and some modern theories of meaninglessness is the idea that dreaming reflects one of the brain's problem-solving operations, a way to analyze the day's activities, process them, and file them away in your mind's many drawers. Dreams then would give you a way to learn about some of the problems your mind is working on.

Rob, twenty-eight years old, tells this story:

> It was the last football game of the season, the second half, and the score was 27 to 7 in favor of the visiting team—in other words, we were getting slaughtered. As quarterback, the pressure was on me to engineer the miracle that would put us ahead. We got a touchdown and the extra point. But time was running out. At the end of the third quarter, we still needed more touchdowns—many more than I had thought. I didn't see how we could win, and I didn't feel I had the energy to go on. I woke up in a sweat.

Rob was in law school when he had this dream of despair. It was his first year, second semester, and the score (to him, anyway) was Rob, falling behind, law school graduation, too far ahead. There was so much more reading than he had time for, and when he was not too exhausted to feel emotion, he feared he would fail the year. When Rob told his dream to his wife, she recognized the parallels between football and law school and decided to give him extra sympathy and support. She was pleased to see that he had associated law school with a game he could quit if he wanted. Rob graduated with honors two years later and is now practicing law in a large bank.

Also through a dream, Jennifer identified some mixed feelings about her long-awaited move from an apartment in the city to a dream house in the country:

> I was in a prison that had windows, the sun streamed in, the furnishings were comfortable, and the door wasn't locked, but I still wasn't allowed to leave. There was nothing to do. No visitors were allowed except my husband.

"I'd been so excited about moving to our new house, but I'd really not dealt with a few facts. We were far from stores that had fresh produce even within reasonable driving distance of our new house," says Jennifer. "And because we'd moved so far out, we had become 'geographically undesirable.' After a few required visits, nobody wanted to come up and see us anymore." Only after she identified the source of her feelings of isolation could Jennifer do something about them. She decided to start a food cooperative to bring good produce within easy access, and she made a few new friends in the process, which took the edge off her loneliness.

Even if you cannot remember your whole dream, you may be able to detect the emotional remnant nonetheless. Ask yourself what emotion you feel when you awaken.

> Vic was moaning in his sleep, in that stifled way that meant he was having a bad dream. His father woke him up and asked him what he was dreaming about. He only remembered that he had seen a mouse with antlers running up the wall, and it had terrified him.

The fearsome mouse with antlers might have represented some piece of a puzzle he was trying to solve, but he never decoded it—which is fine, since he slept very well the following night. But a mutation of a mouse is as good a symbol as any for the negative passions we are so afraid of.

The next four chapters detail four negative passions: despair, fear, rage, and guilt.

Get ready to meet the mouse with antlers!

DESPAIR:
Grief in Brief

3

Despair is not a word many of us use in conversation. We more often invoke despair's sister, depression—"I was so *depressed* because I could not get to the movies last night!" Despair seems to belong more to poetry than to prose, to saints and heroes rather than to our ordinary modern miseries.

And yet we do despair. Despair is a natural response to a major trauma: the loss of a husband, lover, or child; the occurrence of a chronic, incapacitating, or life-threatening illness or injury; for a career-oriented person, the loss of a job. And this reaction is not depression. Though they bear a strong superficial resemblance, despair and depression are far from twins. Recall your last bout and check the following chart to see if you were feeling depression or despair.

DEPRESSION

1.___ I don't know why I feel so bad.
2.___ Nothing I do can cheer me up.
3.___ I feel worse in the morning.
4.___ My movements and speech seem slowed down and I feel like I am dying.
5.___ I sleep a lot more or a lot less than I did before I felt this way.
6.___ I feel that I have let myself down and that I am of little value.

DESPAIR

1.___ A life event triggered my feelings.
2.___ I cry or get teary when I think about that event.
3.___ I feel worse in the evening.
4.___ I wouldn't mind if I died but am not actively considering suicide.
5.___ I feel I'm worth something but life is of little value.
6.___ I feel that the world has let me down.

Depression can occur because of emotional or biochemical forces within, but despair is a response to forces outside of us.

Depression does not vary much, tormenting us as much when we fall asleep as when we awaken, often at the crack of dawn; despair, which sees the world as unfriendly, grows worse in the evenings as the sky darkens.

Depression makes us brood about our health and think about killing ourselves. Despair makes us hope that death will simply take us.

Depression makes us feel helpless and to blame for our misery; despair makes us feel hopeless and as if the world has let us down.

Depression makes us give up on ourselves because we feel that we are not worth much. Despair makes us give up on the world because we feel that life is not worth much.

Depression often makes us too numb to cry; when we do cry, we do not know why. Despair produces emotional tears, and the flow is laden with the chemicals that build up during stress: the hormones prolactin, ACTH (adrenocorticotropic hormone), and leucine-enkephalin (an endorphin, one of the body's natural pain-killers).

The most crucial difference is that whereas depression feels flat, despair is a strongly felt emotion—a passion. Like all tremendous mind/body emotions, despair is a state that will pass, leaving us whole and healthy once more. Depression, in contrast, is a state that can last for years or for a lifetime. The kindest thing you can do for yourself or for a friend in despair is to make sure that the natural anguish felt in response to a blow is not translated into undeserved self-blame—that despair is not allowed to become depression.

Impersonators

Many conditions can mimic despair *and* depression. A physical checkup by an alert, compassionate doctor is especially important when you cannot identify any precipitating event. It may reveal a case of:

anemia
brain damage
virus aftermath (sometimes involves feeling washed out and wiped
    out for long periods)
chronic fatigue syndrome
drug side effects; drug abuse
nutritional deficiencies (especially vitamins B1, B6, and B12)
central nervous system disorders (including multiple sclerosis; some
    brain tumors; strokes)
hormonal disorders
chronic pain
PMS (premenstrual syndrome)

The Birth of Despair

We have very little information on the age at which despair first blooms or whether it is more common in boys or girls, but we do know that it is a lot like distress, the very first negative emotion that babies of either sex show us. A life event—a baby's hunger pang, wet diaper, or absent mother—provokes psychic pain and physical signs, the wailing and flailing we know so well. As we grow, our vocabulary soon expands to include subtle distinctions:

sadness	loneliness
glumness	homesickness
sorrow	defeat
melancholy	dejection
dismay	insecurity
disappointment	embarrassment
displeasure	humiliation
regret	alienation
isolation	

Since we are now finding that children as young as three years of age have symptoms of stress and depression, take your young child's cries of distress as important signals. If there has been a loss in their life, help them through their despair with sympathy and closeness. Asking them to "tough it out" is asking them to teach themselves to be emotionally numb or emotionally isolated. Telling them to "be tough" is adding stress and depression to their despair.

A Woman's Emotion?

In the past, women may have been more vulnerable to despair because they have been "programmed" for it. From the day we were born, females generally received nonassertiveness training.

For example, girls have typically been reared in a more protected way than boys, and this, of course, suggested to us that we *needed* more protection. Girls have been handled more gently, suggesting that we would probably lose in a competition. Boys were taught to fight when something went wrong, girls to control their temper. Boys are supposed to be tough, take-over types; girls are sugar and spice.

Women paid a high price for sugar and spice. The price was often despair. Why? Because we learned not to take control over our lives. We learned that fathers, boyfriends, and husbands made decisions, over which we had little influence. We learned that submissiveness (or at least the appearance of it) rather than achievement or independence (or attempts to gain them) brought us rewards. We learned to be approval junkies, excessively concerned with the opinions of others, so that failure of any kind meant more than personal disappointment—it meant shame. Fear of this shame, this failure, kept many women from any real effort to take control of their own lives, much less any part of the outside world.

How about the new woman who takes charge, against all odds? She runs into the same disappointments as men—plus some. A woman who lands a job *may* find that she is paid less than her male counterpart; that no matter how well she does, she is still considered weaker, less logical, more emotional than a man; that the experience she gains as time goes by is negated by the fact that her aging is held against her. When some major negative event in her life occurs—the loss of a badly needed, cherished job, or being passed over for an expected important promotion, for instance—it may trigger the powerful emotion of despair.

That woman may also find that the men she is working with are not immune to despair. As men have tuned in more to their emotions and to relationships, they have come closer to having many of the same reasons to despair as women have. Men as well as women know despair.

Peter seemed to have everything: two lively children, a wife who gave him love and companionship, a house that was nearly paid for, job security, friends at work and at home. And yet he felt despair because every time he picked up a newspaper or turned on the television, bad news seemed to bombard him. The world seemed out of control, the future seemed perilous. He could not decide whether the solution was to head for the chaos of the streets and fight the trouble, or retreat to his cozy workshop downstairs in the basement, and focus on his family. Day after day, Peter despaired.

Very few respondents in my survey cited despair as their most frequent emotion—only 3.6 percent of men and 0.3 percent of women. But when it did appear, the causes of despair varied: A single thirty-year-old male recreation supervisor felt despair when he watched the TV news or read the paper; a single thirty-one-year-old male student felt despair when alone. Among our few despairing women was a twenty-four-year-old single foreign student who said she despairs when she feels helpless.

Overall, the reasons all male respondents gave for feeling despair were not much different from the reasons women gave: For almost everyone, *loss* is at the core of despair.

Losing a Mate

The loss of a beloved mate has always been commonplace in life, and it is no less painful now than it was a thousand years ago. Here is how two people reacted:

Susan was thirty-four and Neal was thirty-nine. They had invested many nights of fights, years of tears, and hours of therapy in their twelve-year-old marriage. They had learned to please each other and themselves, to share and to care. They still had fights, but basically, they acted bonded and content.

At least, so Susan thought. She was pregnant with their third child when Neal left her. His departure with a woman Susan knew nothing about made no sense to her. For many weeks she awakened each morning believing it had all been a nightmare. When decisions had to be made, she was furious at being bothered with "meaningless details."

When the loss of her husband finally became real to her, Susan's period of despair began. Everything that had happened in the past seemed to have been wasted effort. The future was a bleak desert, equally meaningless. She would rear her children, care for her aging parents, try to make ends meet—all motions to be gone through for no purpose. When her new baby was born, though, the infant's needs began to pull Susan back into the realities of daily life. Small pleasures and even joys appeared. Slowly, Susan began to rebuild.

Slowly, Susan's despair dissolved. Irene's despair did not dissolve—it grew instead.

Irene was fifty-two when Byrne died. Had he lived, Byrne would have celebrated his fifty-fifth birthday and their thirty-fifth anniversary that year. Irene's entire adult life, and part of her teens, had been spent with Byrne. But being told that she was lucky to have so many wonderful years to look back on was not consoling. Irene never contemplated suicide but saw the future only as time to pass through on her way to her own death. She determined never to feel close to anyone again so that she could never again suffer such a loss. She became angry at herself for missing Byrne so much, dwelled morbidly on every minor pain, began to feel helpless and old. Gradually, Irene slipped from an emotional coma of despair into a deep, chronic depression.

In Susan's case, despair served its normal purpose, providing her with a temporary rest from a harsh reality, a time in which her body and spirit were actually dealing with their wound and making ready to recover. In Irene's case, no outside force like a new baby intervened. She lacked the motivation to help herself move on.

Irene, unfortunately, is not unusual—she is one of more than

10 million widows in this country, mostly older women who are unlikely to remarry. A woman's life expectancy is at least six to eight years longer than a man's. This leaves fewer men than women in later years—and, of course, most of those men are already married. The widow's children are usually grown and rearing their own families. For the first time in many years, the widow is without someone to speak to when she awakens, without a social partner during the day and—if she is sexually active—without a lover at night. Since her plight is so common, it does not receive the kind of crisis-inspired social support it deserves. (This is not to say that widowers do not grieve, too; they do, intensely. Studies show that they have fewer friends to talk over their feelings with, and a higher mortality rate than married men of the same age.)

If someone you know has lost a mate, here is how to help him or her pass through despair and into a satisfying reengagement with life:

• Do not overwhelm with advice or interference; this may only threaten self-confidence and prolong despair. Let her formulate her own plans and alternatives. Make yourself available for discussion and fine-tuning of her choices.

• Do not pressure him into social and work activities. Let him know you understand he must mourn his loss and that he is welcome to join you when he is ready. He may feel guilty if he reengages too soon, and this may precipitate depression.

• Do not deny her sorrow or her loss. It is normal for her to feel sorry for herself for a while. Watch for signs that despair is turning to depression rather than to resolution. If she begins to lose weight, to have trouble sleeping, to develop many physical complaints indicating a morbid focus on her health, consult her doctor or seek professional counseling on the next steps to take.

• Do not stay away. Though he may be proud, stoic, or withdrawn, even silent company offers him a needed sense of security and caring.

• If she is experiencing despair of abandonment rather than

widowhood, many of the same precepts apply. Give her time to mourn her loss; offer her companionship even if you do not get much in return. Do not be surprised or alarmed if anguish becomes anger against the runaway mate; this is a normal emotional progression toward adjustment. If the anger is directed inward, help may be required to prevent her from sinking into a depression.

• Do not be surprised if you begin to see that he or she has learned to live alone and even to like it. Both women and men are strong and many ultimately learn to enjoy their own company very much!

Losing a Child

Mourning a child is terribly painful because a child's death violates the natural order. Parents expect to pre-decease their children and make provisions for their death. When a child dies, the shock often prevents a parent from moving through the normal stages of denial, anger, temporary depression, and finally resolution. If a mother or her husband also feel guilt, shame, or blame, these feelings will hold them back from reengagement with life. If the parents were unprepared for the child's death, acceptance and mourning may be even further delayed. If they cannot bear the pain of acknowledging the loss, they may hold on to the magical thinking of denial, the discharging relief of anger, or the numbness of depression.

It was unbelievable to Cynthia that this third pregnancy had just turned into her third miscarriage. No, maybe not unbelievable—in the back of her mind she had been expecting the worst—but she had passed that magic ten-week landmark and was entering her fifth month. How could this baby have been taken away from her now? She had already heard the baby's heartbeat and seen its shadowy shape on a sonogram. Suddenly, she had stopped feeling pregnant, and a follow-up sonogram had shown no life. Tomorrow she would report to the hospital. "I just don't think I can risk having to go through this again," said Cynthia slowly. "Neither can Bart. He's been down in the basement every night this week hammering and sawing—I think it's so he won't have to face me or our problem."

Guilt, shame, shock, and fear of pain can all interfere with the resolution of the loss of a child, even an unborn child. Instead of a sense of closure, a parent will be vulnerable to a general hopelessness about the future and regret about the past. Despair can begin to spread like a blanket across their lives.

How can we help each other and ourselves when the loss is so traumatic? Keep in mind these points:

• Mourning is a must, each in our own way. Attempts to delay or avoid mourning only extend the period of despair that precedes acceptance of the loss.

• A period of despair is not inappropriate when a life has been lost. We must come to terms with the fact that we were not able to control events. Allow for a period of despair.

• A mourning mother or father should have opportunities to talk about grief. They should feel that they have been heard and should receive empathy. As they hear their own words repeated out loud by those who are listening, they will gradually come to take a more objective view of their thoughts and develop a perspective beyond the loss.

• Despair passes. The hopelessness that accompanies the loss of a child gradually becomes less generalized to include all life, and more specific to the event itself. Faith helps some of us, reason helps others, and love helps us all. Cynthia, believe it or not, has convinced her husband that she *does* want to try to conceive again. Her desire for a family returned with a vengeance, surprising even her.

• Unfortunately, the risk of divorce among couples who have lost a child is very high. Couples-counseling with a therapist who has special skills in this area can bring that risk down again. It is important to go to this counseling together and to try to go through the mourning period together!

Losing Your Health

As we grow older, changes in our health—many of them changes for the worse—are normal. We can expect them. We can prepare for them. But when they arrive, what do we do? We resist them with every ounce of strength we have left. Finally, exhausted, we admit that they are here to stay and, perhaps, fall into despair. This is especially likely when health deteriorates unexpectedly.

Caroline was at home one evening when the pain in her chest began. The words *heart attack* crossed her mind—she knew she had high blood pressure and a family history of heart disease, and she was overweight—but then she thought, I'm thirty-three! I'm a woman! It just can't be. Besides, her husband was working his night job and she couldn't have gone anywhere if she wanted to. So she took some antacids. The pain got worse and worse.

By the time Stan got home three hours later, Caroline was ready to go to the hospital. Three days later she was recovering from a bypass operation.

"Talk about despair . . . I wanted to just die," she says now. "Nobody brought flowers—they all brought advice, about exercising, my diet, etcetera, etcetera. I told them all to go away, and I literally sat in bed mourning for myself for a week.

"Even now [five years later] I can't say I've completely recovered emotionally. If this can happen, anything can happen," she says.

Caroline felt robbed of her former life. Her body had betrayed her. Now she felt forced to think of her heart, her weight, her diet, her activity level, and her blood pressure constantly. As you can probably tell, Caroline is still despairing. She has not adjusted very well at all to the requirements of her new life.

We are all human beings riding the cycle of life, and we all fall off at some point. Sometimes health comes back, and sometimes it does not. The loss of health is a serious blow to anybody and everybody. With it comes some loss of choices, loss of control, and loss of our confidence that we can predict what is coming next.

A Tincture of Time

The good news is that because we are all programmed for survival, most of us gradually grow accustomed to the new parameters of our lives. You have to go to the hospital once a week for kidney dialysis? Okay, you can handle that. You cannot put salt on everything the way you used to? You will try parsley. If adjustment comes slowly, thinking about what you get for what you pay may hasten it.

> Joni did not want to have a thyroid tumor. She felt too young for a thyroid tumor—that was an ailment of middle-aged women, and Joni was only thirty-eight. But wait a minute! Thirty-eight *is* middle-aged. Joni was forced to confront her chronological age.
>
> The next blow was that during surgery, a test showed that the tumor was malignant. Now Joni had to confront the concept of having cancer on her once-perfect record of health.
>
> After removing her thyroid gland, the surgeon told Joni she would have to take a pill every day for the rest of her life. But this last straw did not push Joni into despair. She could deal with this because Joni has a four-year-old son. "I'll take a pill every day if that's the price of seeing him grow up," she says. "And I'll try to smile as I swallow each one. They're miracle drugs to me."

Perspective can be a first step in dispelling despair and moving on with life. So look at the big picture when the smaller details are getting in your way.

Situational Despair

An abusive mate, financial troubles, a dead-end job, everyday pressures, the boredom of tasks repeated over and over: these, too, can trigger despair. Life is so impossibly overwhelming that our energy shuts down and allows us the rest we cannot seem to allow ourselves. Here is a story from Bill, who has traded the traditional role of working man for the role of primary caretaker of his children:

> As if it weren't hard enough being a house-husband already! When our two-year-old twin boys get to be pests, it's double the trouble. One morning we all slept late, my wife included, so when she did get up it was, "Where's my breakfast, where's my briefcase, can't you get those kids out of my way?" I don't know how she expected me to keep them from wanting to be with her.
>
> I took the kids into the kitchen with me while I scrambled some eggs. The twins were clinging to my legs. The handle of the frypan chose this moment to come loose, and the pan flipped neatly over, spilling egg onto the floor. While I was trying to clean up the mess, the boys were climbing all over me. I couldn't stand it anymore and began to cry—total despair. Interestingly, though, my outburst slowed everybody down. The boys hugged me around the neck and asked what was the matter, and my wife calmed down too.

Household despair—maybe there should be a whole category devoted to it! Like Bill, the house-husband, you begin to feel that there is no end to the menial tasks you must perform. Worse, you begin to feel that menial tasks are impossible to perform. You know within yourself that you are competent and intelligent, and yet you cannot prepare a meal or keep a confined space neat for more than five minutes. When growing lawns, leaking roofs, finicky furnaces, and accumulating bills become overwhelming, you may be experiencing "household" despair. Like other types of despair, the problem here too is a loss—a loss of your sense of control and of your self-esteem.

Are there ways to dig out of this daily despair? Yes, and they work for other types of situational despair, too:

First, you must not allow your situation to pass judgment on you.

A toy on the floor is not a verdict on your housekeeping abilities, and a large insect in the kitchen is not necessarily a reflection on your cleanliness. Both can be seen as life's "inconveniences" rather than *your* failures.

Second, keep that competence and intelligence inside you alive! List all the things you *can* do. If you have forgotten how to do them, resurrect them. It is important.

Finally, look at your life in long-term perspective. Household despair, for example, often involves the noises and illnesses of children. One day those children will probably no longer be living with you and it may seem hard to imagine, but one day you may yearn for a two-year-old to hang on to your legs. Once again the big picture puts the daily details in their place.

Another strategy that may help is to draw an imaginary circle around a difficult situation and contain it emotionally within the circle. Now the situation is in its place; you have put some distance between it and yourself. Now you may be able to think about it more objectively as you go about the rest of your life.

Dealing with Despair

How do we break the pattern of fear of failure and therefore of responsibility? How do we break this cycle of inaction, the loss of the sense of control, the hopelessness and despair? Here are three powerful steps to take.

• Learn to make more decisions. Make choices when they are offered to you, even on trivial things: Do not say, "I don't care, it's up to you." Take the choice even if you *don't* care. Create choices for yourself, especially when you begin to feel hopeless, and soon you'll begin to feel that you are a life force again. And if it's fear of failure that keeps you from making decisions, you need more practice making mistakes. In fact, if you aren't making at least two mistakes each day, you probably aren't taking enough risks to avoid despair.

• Look at the world through *your* eyes rather than looking at yourself through the world's eyes. Remember that unless you have the gift of telepathy, trying to see yourself as someone else sees you just does not work. You *do not* know what someone else is thinking.

• Keep in mind that life is a package deal. Sad, even tragic, losses over which we have no control will inevitably occur. Accidents, illnesses, and deaths will happen; beauty fades in time; things change. Remember that these are facts of life, not punishments inflicted on you because you are a bad person.

• Since it is impossible to feel a negative and a positive emotion at the same time, one way to get rid of despair is to try to get involved in activities that make you feel good. You might:

sing or listen to music	plan a short trip
have lunch with a friend	call up an old friend
buy yourself something nice	visit the zoo
visit a museum	take a walk

These activities will not solve your problems or take away the source of your despair, but by treating yourself well, you will give yourself at least a little lift, see a different side of life for a short while, relate to yourself in a loving way, and give your inner resources a chance to regenerate.

After Despair

Despair has a purpose, and then it passes. It is usually just one stage in a readjustment process. Usually, this readjustment involves our incorporating a loss or tragedy into our view of life. We learn that our dear ones can and do die or leave us, that we can be badly disappointed, that we can lose the security, the routines, the expectations, the control, and the self-esteem that help give us our sense of identity. We learn that all this happens, and yet we survive and can even be happy again.

Unfortunately, despair does not always pass into this new realism. If we confuse these external events with internal ineffectiveness on our own part, we may drift into depression. According to Nancy K. Schlossberg, Ph.D., first director of the American Council on Education, Office of Women, this is most apt to happen if:

• a loss or tragedy occurs *out of phase* rather than at a more expected time; for example, if you have become a widow at age thirty, have breast cancer at age twenty, become pregnant at age sixteen.

• a loss or tragedy is *permanent* rather than temporary.

• a loss or tragedy *follows closely* behind others. There seems to be a cumulative effect when negative events cluster together. Both physiologically and psychologically, our resources become exhausted and the risk of depression increases.

• a loss or tragedy is *experienced alone*. The support of a spouse, family, friends, or agencies is important to the prevention of depression, offering empathy, encouraging health care and rest, and hastening reinvolvement with structured and social activities.

If you are trying to help someone through a period of despair, keep track of five important signs.

1. *The intensity of her feelings*: The more her despair interferes with her work, social life, and self-image, the more serious it is.
2. *The length of time it lasts*: The longer the duration, the more risk there is of chronic depression.
3. *The precipitating event*: If you can identify a specific event, the low period is more likely to pass.
4. *Hallucinations, delusions, sleep disturbances, weight loss, or suicidal threats, fantasies or attempts*: If any of these occur, consult a mental health specialist immediately.
5. *Dependency needs that go up, decision-making abilities that go down, disorganization, and forgetfulness*: These are frequent signs of situa-

tional stress, and may even be indicating that the despair is temporary and will resolve. Be patient.

If it is not your mother, your father, or your friend who is in despair but you, let your family and friends help you. Your loss or hurt may not be reversible, but the deep emptiness in your life can be refilled. Allow the healing process the time it requires. Let yourself love and be loved. Remember that life brings joy as well as grief. Both are human, and both are part of your life.

FEAR:
The Runaway Emotion

4

$\approx$

Remember the monster who lived under your bed when you were little? Or maybe he hid in the closet, in the crawl space, in the cellar—*somewhere* dark. What did he mean, and why did you fear him? He symbolized fear, and you feared him because fear is something all children feel. By creating an effigy of fear, you could practice fearing in a safe situation. At the same time that you were totally terrified of this strange creature, you knew that it existed only in your mind. Practice is one way that children prepare for life in the world.

Fun Fear

The *Wizard of Oz*, with its witches and haunted woods, is one of the favorite movies of all time. The movies *Halloween* and *Friday the 13th* have had many sequels. In one town, a youth group puts on a Halloween haunt—a spook house—in the "crypt," a basement, and children who want to come through can sign up for the "mild" tour, the "scary" tour, or the "superscary" tour. Go to an amusement park and watch the kids stagger down the off-ramp of a wild roller coaster ride. "Wow, that was really scary!" they say.

Why would anyone deliberately pursue a scary experience? It is a way to test your strength: I was afraid, I came out of it alive—not only alive but *triumphant.* T-shirts proclaim evolutionary superiority of all kinds: I survived the cyclone; I survived a trip to New York. Watching movies, touring haunted houses, and riding roller coasters are relatively safe ways to be scared.

Children practice overcoming real fears, too. In one study of 1,700 ninth-grade boys and girls, both sexes were united in their fear of darkness and unknown people. Girls were particularly afraid of insects, injury, death, and being alone; boys were more concerned with unknown animals and heights. Boys cope with fears by desensitizing themselves; they confront the fear again and again until it holds no power over them. They plunge into the dark cemetery or jump off the high dive—and take care to appear very nonchalant each time they do, until they really are. Boys care very much what other boys think of them, so they often use others' opinions to push them into confrontation with their fears. Even before they enter nursery school, boys are fighting bad guys, blasting ghosts and monsters, and "killing" each other with pretend guns made of sticks.

Girls handle their fear a different way: They tend to look for support in other people. It is easy to imagine a little girl running to mother or a teacher for help or comfort and much less easy to imagine a little boy doing that. In high school, a girl who is afraid may turn to a boy for protection. It is almost a ritual. Does the high school girl who finds a spider in her locker kill it herself? Not if there's a boy nearby. She screams and begs the nearest boy to do it. A classic strategy. Or remember Olive Oyl? Each time Bluto threatened her, Popeye would save her, and she would say adoringly, "Oh, *Pop*eye!" as cartoon hearts bloomed in the sky. Traditionally, girls have been encouraged to abdicate the right to confront their biggest fears and have looked for ways to share and dilute them instead.

Today's young girls have more chances to develop a tradition of bravery. For both sexes, sports are a wonderful chance to conquer fear and establish personal power. When coaches say that playing sports builds character, they know what they are talking about. In sports, a boy or girl is shown an obstacle—a long-jump mark, a hurdle, a time to beat, an opposing field hockey team, a huge opponent. Then through effort, strategy, and attack, that boy or girl sets out to surmount the obstacle and defeat the enemy. When he or she fails to do so, it might be agonizing, but it is normal. After all, in sports defeat happens. Losing in sports shows young people what happens after fear: not death or shame, but simple acknowledgment and dignity.

Fear and Survival

Fear has survival value for us before we are old enough to say its name. For a young child, fear is anyone who is not Mommy, Daddy, or someone very familiar. This may be nature's way of making sure that the child picked up by a stranger (or, in the earlier days of our evolution, a wild animal) sounds a loud alarm.

Fear makes us uncomfortable because it takes over psychologically and physically. We can focus on nothing but the thing we fear. Our heart rate goes up, we breathe more rapidly, we perspire—the fight-or-flight response kicks in. Fear takes advantage, usually, of the flight part. Even in fear's milder forms—tenseness, uneasiness, anxiety—your muscles tighten and you can feel adrenaline calling for you to escape the uncomfortable situation. At fear's most intense—alarm, panic, horror, hysteria—we run, we scream, our stomach gets upset. We are barely in control. Rob, a twenty-eight-year-old father, tells of a brush with fear:

Here's a sight I hope you never see—a Fourth of July rocket spiraling straight toward you and your family. We were all sitting on the stoop for the fireworks display my father puts on every year. But though he is a brilliant scientist—a rocket scientist, no kidding—he's an amateur with fireworks. Anyway, Dad set off a few sparklers and rockets and everyone oohed and aahed. Then he gets out another rocket, points it straight up, lights the fuse, the rocket rises—and then the silly thing slowly arcs over and begins spiraling toward us. I'd been nervous, so I was already on my feet and out of the way fast, and my wife moved quickly too. But my mother, my sister, and her little girl were frozen. My wife was screaming to them, "RUN! RUN! RUN!" and they just couldn't move. It was only luck that the rocket came in about five feet over their heads. Then it hit the door, fell onto the stoop, and burned its way into the wall.

Why were three of the five people sitting on those steps unable to move? Probably because in the wild, freezing and blending into the scenery like a squirrel or rabbit is a way to avoid detection. Like the fight-and-flight response, this response to fear also has survival value. Imagine yourself lost on the subway. You finally decide to get out and ask directions. You realize quickly that you are not only in an unfamiliar neighborhood but that an angry-looking man muttering aloud to himself is not twenty feet away. He has not seen you yet; you freeze behind a column, and he passes by without seeing you. Survival value? You are counting on it.

Fear as Teacher

Whether we flee or freeze, fear in any of its forms makes us uncomfortable because it is such an intense emotion. On top of that, the *thing* we fear makes us feel uncomfortable, small, weak, and trapped. Sometimes fear leaves an indelible mark on us. In my survey, I asked men and women about their first memory of fear. The memories reached far back into childhood: a first haircut, not having done their homework, a beating by a father, a nightmare, early surgery.

Because it is so memorable, fear is a good teacher. Not the best teacher: Repetition, explanation, and motivation work, too, and they are much kinder and gentler than the punishment that fear is. Psychologists define punishment as a stimulus that an experimental subject does not enjoy. The feeling of fear is so unpleasant to many of us that we are happy to take whatever action is necessary to avoid it. Our ancestors learned to stay away from the trail that led past the bear's cave. At least one modern family avoids fireworks displays. The child makes sure his homework is done next time before he is called on to recite. The mother learns to watch her child more intently:

> Since my husband doesn't like yard work, I do it all myself, and that's not easy with a two-year-old you have to watch every minute. One summer afternoon, I desperately wanted to finish cutting the grass so I could say I'd finished one thing that day. All that was left was a section next to the road. Jason wouldn't stay in the driveway so I took him with me, holding his hand. In the one second that I let go of him to push the lawn mower over a hump, Jason stepped into the street. A car was there, and the poor woman behind the wheel slammed on her brakes. The car screeched, I screeched, Jason froze . . . it was horrifying. Luckily, I had enough presence to snatch him out of the way. I apologized to the woman and carried Jason into the house so I could sit down. That was when I began to shake and cry.

After a good scare, we say "Never again!" and will do almost anything to make sure that is the truth.

Some fears are idiosyncratic—they seem to come on for no historic or logical reason. Two others are appropriate and justified— the fear of physical harm and the fear of another's harm.

Fear of Physical Harm

Fear of physical harm can have a fascinating effect on us. We can experience heightened awareness and clarity of sensation. It can boost our ability to think about what is going to happen and allow us to save ourselves. As we react in double time, real time seems to slow.

It was a snowy afternoon, and fifteen-year-old Dennis and a friend were on the way to a movie. His friend's mother was driving. As they rounded a curve to the left, they saw a startling sight: a car sliding toward them, out of control, clearly not able to negotiate the curve on the slippery road. The car was on a collision course with the car Dennis was in.

Dennis can still describe the faces he saw years ago in that car as he watched it drift slowly (or so it seemed to him) across the center line. "A man was driving, and he was not even trying to steer anymore—he was frozen, just gripping the wheel," he says. "His face was full of tension. Next to him was an old lady who was so frightened I could see the lines of her neck muscles.

"I knew that since I had not put on my seat belt I might go through the windshield, so I very methodically raised my knees and positioned them between myself and the dashboard. I put my right hand on the door handle and the left one out in front of me." In the crash that followed, Dennis's knees were badly bruised and cut. That was all. In what had been in reality probably fractions of a second, Dennis had taken thoughtful, sensible action to save himself.

The adrenaline that our adrenal glands pump out in response to fear can work two ways: In smaller quantities, it clears our mind and makes way for exactly the right action, as in Dennis's case. In larger quantities, though, it floods the reasoning faculties and logic deteriorates.

Most of us do not think of fear of physical harm unless we must, when we are ill or threatened. For most of us, that is not very often. We think even less often of fear of death. When we do acknowledge death's power over us, it can be overwhelming. Fear of death is natural, an emotion we can accept as a healthy part of ourselves, a reluctance for most of us to leave life.

Fear of Another's Harm

That we can become afraid when another person is threatened is a testament to the greatness of human love. We can love other people so much that their pain becomes our own. Mothers enter burning buildings to save their children; husbands step in front of onrushing trucks to push their wives out of the way. It is so natural that when it is over and the newspaper reporters ask how it felt to take such heroic action, the person who saved the lives claims to not even have thought twice about it.

If it is clear that saving someone else holds no immediate survival value for us, why has this trait survived human evolution? First, when we save our children, we save our genes if not ourselves directly. Second, when we save *anybody*, we are working with the human race and not against it. If we help when others are in need, it is more likely they will help when we are in need. However calculated it may seem, to help other people is to help ourselves.

Fear of Criticism

Many other fears are not so life-threatening as physical harm, but they can threaten our well-being. Many people fear criticism, which has as its basis a loss of love or respect, with its inherent threat of humiliation, punishment, rejection, or being cast out of the group.

Christine was flattered to have been chosen for the debating team, but now that the first debate was seconds from beginning, she wondered what her teammates had seen in her and what had made her accept their invitation. As she sat waiting for the opening gambit, she tried not to look at the sea of faces in the audience.

The pro side started first, then came her side; the pro people had another turn, and now it was Christine's moment of truth. Her heart was pounding as she rose and began to present her argument. As she spoke, she felt her throat tighten. She continued speaking even though her voice had begun to sound quite peculiar. Soon her throat was so constricted she was unable to produce a sound. She looked around, panicked, as the silence lengthened.

Although not everyone is afflicted with a profound terror of public speaking, many, many people sympathize with those who are. Fear of public speaking has been reported to be America's number-one phobia. In this cliffhanger of a moment, Christine searched the faces she could see clearly in the glare of the lights—and found friends. The faculty adviser smiled and made a "go on, go on" gesture with his hands; her teammates' eyes were soft with shared feeling; even the opposing team waited politely, without the glee Christine expected to find in their expressions. Christine determined to collect herself. She swallowed the lump in her throat, took a deep breath, and picked up her argument where she had left off. Afterward, she received compliments on the logic of her presentation.

Christine was clearly competent and up to the job before her. Why did she choke? Because she began to look at herself through everyone else's eyes. She felt that her insecurities were as visible as the nose on her face. We know that *we* talk about other people, so we expect them to judge us, too.

One way to neutralize a fear of criticism is to stop criticizing *yourself*. Self-criticism suggests to others that you are worth criticizing, and it often becomes a self-fulfilling prophecy. If you are criticizing yourself about an error, remember that time will pass and the error will fade in importance.

Another way to dissolve a fear of criticism is to focus on the work at hand rather than on yourself. Look out at the world through *your own eyes*, not through everyone else's eyes. If you are completely caught up in town politics, you *will* be able to knock on doors and ask people to sign a petition. If you really believe in animal rights, you *will* be able to appear on a televised panel discussion to defend your views. If you really care about the future of your synagogue, you *will* be able to stand up in front of a gathering and make a case for large donations.

Finally, as we have said so many times before, practice. Find a place where you feel safe—say, at your dressing table, in front of the mirror—and practice until you feel completely confident. Then practice in front of one friend, then the family, and finally an audience. Ignore any signs of nervousness. Think of them as minor inconveniences. Soon confidence will become the first reaction.

Fear of Failure

In my Passions Survey, I found that more people feared failure than anything else. They feared "not living up to my potential" (a twenty-eight-year-old adviser); "not succeeding in my goals" (a thirty-six-year-old male social worker); "finding out that I'm really stupid" (a forty-two-year-old secretary); and simply "failure" (nine men and women of all ages and walks of life).

We are hard on ourselves. It seems we lack the confidence to pursue our own interests. We judge ourselves on performance and expect to be judged by others.

Of course, a fear of failure can be channeled positively as a motivation to succeed. If this fear mobilizes you rather than immobilizes you, it is an appropriate emotion. If it serves no other purpose in life than to torture you, put your mind to work to get rid of it.

Nobody in my survey cited a fear of success, but it is real for many women who have been raised in traditional families, where men make the important decisions and women abide by them. What will happen to a woman if she becomes the decision maker? That has been a source of fear for many women over the last decades and still is for some.

Joni had been having elevator dreams ever since she was five years old and a department store elevator door had closed between Joni and her mother and separated them. When she became an adult, elevators were a symbol of her growing away from her parents and of her ambitions, her desire to rise in the world. Should she accept the major promotion she had just been offered? Of course, Joni's conscious mind said. A dream showed her that she may not have been as sure as she thought.

> *Joni was standing in the elevator as it began to go up, but there were no sides on the elevator, so she could see the land and people dropping away as the elevator rose. Joni was terrified and began to scream, so loudly that her ears rang with the sound of it. The ascent lasted a long time. Then the elevator slowly rose into a sunny attic room, all carpeted and furnished in white. The elevator stopped and Joni stepped out. A beautiful bed was a few steps away, with fluffy white pillows and an eyelet coverlet, waiting just for her.*

Joni thought the dream meant she was working out a conflict about the job. She felt she wanted to take the job but also to curl up in a safe bed in a safe little girl's room instead. She finally decided she could have both wishes because she eventually would be very comfortable in the job, which turned out to be true.

Success sounds good but may look frightening to the woman for whom it is a change. Success may mean you will threaten some men. It will also mean that you will earn your own money and have some personal power. Your husband or father will no longer be your employer. He will no longer feel he has the right to say, "Damnit, where's my shirt?" to you or use your name like a curse word. If you fear that your independence will lead to abandonment—a fear often expressed in my survey—ask yourself whether it might not be a change for the better. If you fear it may lead you to more responsibility, ask yourself whether it, too, might be worth it.

Fear of Loss

In her novel *Dinner at the Homesick Restaurant*, Anne Tyler takes the voice of a mother who loves her first baby so intensely that she decides she needs to have another one in case something happens to the first. Then she finds out she loves that one intensely, too.

After the third baby, she realizes she has multiplied her terror by three.

This mother feared that her child would be harmed, but she also felt a more selfish emotion; when another person is taken from us, we feel the pain. Because we are set up to love each other deeply, a loss is a deeply felt pain, one that we dread.

> Randy's dad had been sick for a while, and it was serious: He was not expected to survive this illness. Randy and his brothers were already feeling the pain of losing him, an acute pain that made it hard for all of them to laugh, work, or enjoy life. They could not adjust to the idea that one day he would not be with them.
>
> Then Randy's father died. "How could you stand the pain?" a friend asked Randy. "You stand it," said Randy. "I had to accept his death. There was nothing we could do. He was here, then he left, and we miss him terribly. That's all there is to it."

According to my Passions Survey, both men and women spend a good deal of time fearing the loss of people they love. Some of the time, it is useful practice; since we will all lose people we love unless we die first. Examining pain before it actually arrives can prepare us, as it did Randy. Fear of loss becomes inappropriate, however, when the time we spend in dread is for no reason: A loved one is not even sick or in danger, and you are already grieving so hard you cannot do your work and take care of yourself. Since we all die, fear of death is a wasted emotion. If your fear of loss has immobilized you, hang your black mourning garb back in the closet until you really need it, and focus on the life of the living. You know how precious others are to you; tell them about it now! Spend time with them now. Avoid future regrets.

Jealousy

Jealousy is a hybrid emotion: part fear of loss, part anger. The recipe also calls for a pinch of low self-esteem—because if you were perfectly confident about yourself, you would probably not feel jealousy. Love's curse, it has been called.

> Jeannie loved parties. At parties she always did the same thing: She talked with lots of people, large and small, male and female, local or foreign—she just loved the scene. Most of her dates found this acceptable and normal. Not Wayne. To his understanding, she was his for the evening; she should make her jokes for him, drink her drink with him, smile her smile for him. When Jeannie did all of these things without him, Wayne took personal offense and decided to end the evening. In the car, he told her angrily that he had seen her flirting and that if she ever expected to go out with him again, she had better remember who her date was.

A frightening character, this Wayne, and Jeannie decided *not* to go out with him again. She was smothered by his possessiveness. If you frequently feel jealous of people under far-ranging circumstances, then this kind of fear is part of the way *you* react, and it is probably making your emotional life bumpy. Telling people you are jealous tells them you do not trust them, and a good relationship cannot be built on fear and mistrust.

If you frequently feel jealously fearful with the same person, consider that jealousy can be a good barometer of a relationship. Does your boyfriend flirt at parties? Does your husband load himself with so many outside activities and commitments that you feel jealous of what he is doing? Something is wrong: Either your trust level is off, or the other person really does prefer outside company. Look into it.

Managing Fears

It is fair to say that nobody wants more fear in his or her life. Here are five ways to exorcise it:

• *Get rid of anticipatory fear.* It unnecessarily doubles our dose of fear, and we do it to ourselves! If you catch yourself becoming terrified of future situations that never may come to pass, try *passive acceptance*. Say to yourself, "If it happens, it happens." Do not fight the future's phantoms. Refocus on the present problems.

• *Take control.* If your hall stairs scare you—when you stand at the top of the stairway and look down at all those hard steps— consider having them carpeted or putting an area rug at the bottom. If your boyfriend's temper scares you, speak with him about it or arrange for him to get help. Or, if you must, help yourself and get away. Put yourself in the center of your world and take action to gather what you need around *you*.

• *Change your reaction.* Many people are able to actually turn down the volume of their fear response. One way to do this is to behave *as if* you are not fearful. If you don't make use of your fear, soon you will produce less of it. Another way to do this is by *progressive desensitization* which we spoke about earlier: Simply put, you first confront a watered-down version of the source of your fear. If you are afraid of spiders, you might start with a mental image of a spider that does not even make you cringe. Make a conscious effort to relax as you picture the spider, because relaxation is a positive emotion, fear is a negative emotion, and as we now know, the two cannot exist simultaneously. The next object you confront in your fear hierarchy might be a photo of a tiny spider, then a larger spider, until you can relax in front of each. Then try the real thing. Progressive desensitization is often the approach of choice for phobics, people with irrational fears.

• *Think your way out.* Psychological researcher Aaron Beck, the father of cognitive psychology, theorized that emotions are blendings of thoughts and feelings. For example, uneasiness plus thoughts of harm lead to fear. It is possible to dissect almost any emotional reaction into manageable parts. In cognitive therapy, you deal one by one with the thoughts that combine with feelings to make you emotionally overwhelmed. Separately, each is underwhelming. Let's use the example of a fear of spiders again. By altering how we view something cognitively, we can tell ourselves spiders are small. We can tell ourselves they rarely do any harm. We can consciously look into our own histories to see why we fear them. We can see them as tiny facts of life—like ants and flies.

• *Analyze fear in progress.* As you feel the spine-tingling desire to run away come over you, take the opportunity to recognize the cause of your fear. There is no better time. First, cut through your feelings of panic and identify the fear. Is it legitimate? If it is, use your rational state of mind to decide what to do: to dodge an onrushing car; to have a mammogram because you feel a lump in your breast; to take the knife away from your child; to assess your chances of escaping from a rapist. If your fear is not legitimate—you are anticipating fear, for example, or you fear success—choose to compartmentalize these useless fears and reassign the energy you would have spent on fear.

There is one more thing to remember about fear: It can be useful. Fear is often a measure of danger in our lives, and it can save us. So assess each fear and decide if it is a life-saving fear or a fear from which your life needs saving!

RAGE:
Anger in Action

5

Your heart is pounding, and your blood pressure is rising. Your eyes are bright and your pupils dilated. Your fists are clenched, and your teeth are, too. You're not in love. You are enraged.

Rage is more than anger. It is anger *plus* an impetus for immediate action. Anger can be dwelled upon, but rage demands to be acted upon. Anger can be all in the mind, but rage is unmistakably physical, too. Anger can last and last, but rage must pass as the body's fight-or-flight system becomes exhausted. While we are actually in the powerful grip of rage, however, we do not think it will ever pass.

As the brain reacts to an infuriating event, the autonomic nervous system is aroused. Adrenaline, released from the adrenal glands, begins to pour into the bloodstream, increasing heart rate and respiration and stimulating the release of stored sugars for energy. We are ready for action, feeling tireless and invincible. We go into action with an all-consuming passion we know will seem as logical and appropriate later on as it does now. Unfortunately for us, it often does not. Which of the following are true for you?

1. I get annoyed when someone cuts in front of me at a toll booth line.
2. I feel annoyed when someone else steals credit for my work.
3. Getting overloaded with someone else's work makes me mad.
4. I often get furious when I'm kept waiting at a doctor's office.
5. I frequently hold grudges and try to get even.
6. I get angry every day.

If you said yes to questions 1 through 3, your rage response is normal. If you said yes to questions 4 through 6, your rage response is very sensitive, perhaps oversensitive.

Actions we take under the influence of our own adrenaline are often overreactions. You can see it in its purest form in a child. In the first years, the child becomes enraged when the world does not always do or act the way the child would like. For example, the baby would like to play with the shiny scissors, and Mommy takes them away. The baby screams, the baby cries, the baby flails, the baby gets red in the face. By two years of age and experience, a child has learned more about reality. But she now wants to assert her autonomy. Her favorite word becomes *no*. "Time to go to bed now," we say. "No!" says the toddler. We repeat our request, and soon the toddler could be on the floor, kicking, pounding, screaming, and crying—adrenaline made visible.

Most parents do not allow a display like this to push bedtime back one minute because that would teach the child that kicking, pounding, screaming, and crying get results. But at the same time, most of us know that we must deal with the physical side of rage.

> Matthew is a normal three-year-old boy who is learning words and singing nursery rhymes. His friend Carter is a three-year-old genius: He can read any book, pick out tunes on his little piano— and outsmart any of his peers. It particularly amuses Carter to frustrate Matthew, probably as a test of his emerging powers. One summer day, the boys were out playing in Matthew's blue plastic pool. "It's not a pool, it's a tub," says Carter.
>
> "It's a pool," says Matthew.

"Tub," says Carter.

"Pool!" says Matthew.

"Tub," says Carter.

"POOL!" says Matthew.

"Tub," says Carter.

"POOL! POOL! POO-OO-OO-OO-OOL!" screams Matthew, and bursts into tears. He is so enraged he is shaking. His mother has heard the conversation through the kitchen window and rushes out. She takes a stick from Matthew that he is about to throw at Carter. Matthew runs away screaming.

Even when adulthood arrives, we are still becoming enraged; we scream, hurl hateful semi-truths, hit, damage, destroy, or leave the scene in a huff. We are then left with the job of trying to rationalize our behavior to ourselves and to others. How much worth the effort it would be to interrupt the escalation of hostility before rage and its excuses begin.

RAGE REPORT

Have you ever lost your temper? Check off the excuses you have used after the fact:

A. ___ What I did wasn't as bad as what I *might* have done.

B. ___ I didn't start it. It wasn't *my* fault.

C. ___ The way I behaved was wrong, but it *worked.*

D. ___ He/she *deserved* it.

E. ___ He/she isn't worth bothering about, so it *doesn't matter.*

F. ___ I only *behaved the same way* he/she did.

G. ___ *Everybody* does the same thing.

H. ___ It's *healthier* to let rage out.

I. ___ I *warned* them, but they didn't listen.

In a book called *Aggression*, Albert Bandura, Ph.D., of Stanford University, analyzes many of these rationalizations for our irrational rage behavior.

If you checked A, you are drawing comparisons between real behavior and potential behavior. Rage behavior can escalate over time, so this excuse can become a self-fulfilling prophecy. Take it as a warning instead. Has your rage behavior already gotten worse?

If you checked B, F, G, or I, you are trying to displace responsibility. Unfortunately, this usually goes along with a tendency to let others run your life. If we must live with the consequences of our rage, we might as well take responsibility for it—and then do something about the situation that caused it.

If you checked C, you are claiming that the end justifies the means. World wars have been fought on this rationalization—why not personal battles? In any personal relationship, rage behavior builds up a shared negative history. In other words, the enraged person makes her point, but the relationship is permanently altered for the worse.

If you checked D or E, you are rationalizing. This rationalization only helps us avoid examining our aggressive behavior. Women should be particularly sensitive to this type of excuse for rage because it has been used against us for so long.

If you checked H, you are saying, "Let it all hang out." Have you noticed the consequences? Aside from the rage habit that you may be developing, you may have observed that those who are around when you let it all out are usually moved to angry reprisals, withdrawal of love, or defensiveness. Instead of a catharsis that reduces hostility, you now have a situation that perpetuates your rage.

Get a Grip on Rage

Why is it so difficult to control rage? Here are some of the reasons:

Modeling   We imitate behavior that seems to work for someone else. Every time a child is physically punished, she learns not only what enrages her parents but how to express her own rage. There is a direct correlation between physical punishment of children and their aggressive behavior and even between children's seeing rage behavior in real life or in a film and how they behave toward dolls and each other a few minutes afterward.

Desensitization   Repeated exposure to rage lowers our threshold for the expression of rage. This is true for the daughter whose mother constantly yells, the boy whose friends constantly fight, and the soldier whose company constantly kills. The stimulus, rage, becomes associated with the response, aggression. Every time the stimulus-response sequence is rehearsed, the connection gets stronger and self-control gets weaker. This is called the *practice effect*, and it holds true for all emotions.

Frustration   The adrenaline of rage seeks an immediate outlet. Although our mind may be responding more rationally, an enraged body is primed for retaliation, and going through channels or biding our time seems to require too much control. They are beyond our tolerance. Do you remember the last oil shortage? Do you remember how many fights there were among car drivers lined up at the gas pumps? Frustration made adrenaline flow, and those drivers were primed for fight or flight. They couldn't leave their cars (flight), so many used up the adrenaline by hitting each other (fight).

Distance   The few natural inhibitors we humans have to keep us from killing each other work only at close range. They are face-to-face signals: sobs, tears, and words. At long range they do not work. If an aggressor is facing a missile button rather than a human victim, empathy will not be activated and pushing the button will be easy. A philosopher once proposed an interesting solution. In order to set missiles flying, the president would have to push a button, but the button would be embedded deeply in the chest of a man or woman. To get to the button, the president would have to open the person's chest with a knife. This brings home the fact that long-distance aggression is too easy.

Accumulation   Years of nonassertiveness training give many women a store of unexpressed anger. If it continues to build long enough, the final explosion may be dramatic. To the world it seems to come out of nowhere; to the woman who has been trying to keep her aggression under control, it reflects a long, slow burn finally bursting into flames. It is often the logical end of a chain of events that involve earlier forms of anger or anger in disguise, such as:

aggravation	loathing	outrage
irritation	spite	envy
agitation	vengefulness	hostility
annoyance	dislike	jealousy
grouchiness	resentment	bitterness
grumpiness	disgust	torment
exasperation	revulsion	hate
frustration	contempt	

. . . and, of course, anger itself. In Justine's story, you can see several of these precursors before she erupts into rage.

Justine woke up late. Three weeks earlier she had taken a bad fall and her back still ached; every morning she felt as tired as if she had not slept. On the subway she pushed into a crowded car with standing room only. "Standing room? Standing *no room!*" she muttered to herself. Two pokes and a shove later she pushed her way out again. It had begun to rain. Wet and weary, Justine entered her office in the high school where she served as principal. A delinquent student was already in her anteroom, a budget-cut notice was on her desk, her secretary was out sick, and her phone was ringing. On the other end was an officer of the co-op building she wanted to live in; he was calling to say her application had been turned down.

Justine saw red. Her hands shook, her knees shook, her voice shook. She slammed down the receiver and screamed at the student in the waiting room. All day she could not sit still. Her rage consumed her.

Although the final provocation was being turned down for an apartment, Justine was already primed to overreact. She was tired and in pain; she had been crowded, inconvenienced, overloaded, and finally presented with an unexpected disappointment beyond her control. Justine's case illustrates an important principle: A rage reaction is more likely after wear-and-tear on our coping system.

Rage as Result

Even without lowered resistance, most of us respond to one or more of the following situations with an outburst of fury:

Intrusions into our physical or psychological space. Think of the rage that follows a robbery, an obscene phone call, an uninvited sexual advance. How *dare* they, we think afterward, obsessively, furiously, for many days.

Or consider what happened when Bill inadvertently trespassed on Susan's psychological territory.

Susan had planned the board meeting so it would not run past 11 P.M. But it did, and Bill, a new member, said in a lecturing voice, "I have a complaint. My time is valuable, and there is no reason at all—at all!—for a meeting to run on so."

Susan was infuriated. He was attacking her and her meeting. She felt her mind and body gear up for action. Her thoughts became crystal clear, and within seconds she was responding, "Bill, *you* can walk out of here at any time. In this meeting *we* make decisions as a group, and we're not finished yet." She then pushed through three short items and requested a motion for adjournment—from Bill.

But that night she lay in bed, reliving the run-in, her fists clenched with rage. How dare he challenge her publicly! At 2:30 she took a bath and read a hundred pages of a novel. At 4:30 she drank a glass of milk. She was still awake at 6:30 when the alarm-clock radio came on.

Threats that may be followed by pain can trigger a giant rage. Have you ever been enraged by a driver whose carelessness could have involved you in an accident? Your rage is a response to a threat. Have you ever responded with rage when a lover tried to leave a relationship? This too is a response to a threat, the threat of a painful separation, the pain of loss.

> Neil had finally reached his conclusion: He was not ready for marriage. Unfortunately, his bride-to-be had already bought her wedding dress, and many other arrangements were well under way.
>
> Neil chose his words carefully, but they did not matter; Lois was terribly sad, wounded—and enraged. She alternately screamed, cried, and pounded his chest. With her bare hands, she tore up a straw hat of hers that he had liked. Then she ran out of the apartment to her car, where she cried for two hours before finally driving off.

Luckily, Lois's wedding dress was not nearby, or she would have snipped that to shreds as well! It is a good thing she did not, because she wore it at her wedding three years later.

Injuries to our self-image or to those with whom we identify can cause rage. This is why we startle ourselves with the passion with which we defend a political candidate, a friend, a spouse, or ourselves.

Attacks on our children, actual or implied, behavioral or emotional, can call out our rage. Most women become livid with anger when they hear about child abuse; most feel they could actually kill to defend their own children.

Impediments that frustrate our progress toward an important goal can cause rage. For teenagers, this means rage at parents who seem to be interfering with their progress toward independence. For divorced people, it can mean rage at the ex-spouse who limits their mobility or financial well-being. For a wife it can mean rage at a husband who insists her place is somewhere she would prefer not to be.

Disappointments that are unexpected or seem unjustified can trigger rage. Justine, the school principal, was pushed over the edge of control into rage by an arbitrary and irrevocable decision that dramatically lowered her sense of control and choice. Such disappointments make us feel victimized and furious.

Why do we have the capacity for rage? In primitive societies, the rage response was probably vital for survival. The physiological changes in heart rate and respiration prepared us to fight for territory, ward off trespassers, compete for mates or food, protect our young, overcome fear, ignore pain, and punish wrongdoers. But once tribes replaced bands and villages replaced tribes, institutions rather than individuals took over the management of territoriality, mating, food distribution, and criminal justice. Civilization now demands that individual rage reactions be channeled through social systems.

What do we do with our rage? Usually, the wrong things. We are often so uncomfortable with our angry impulses that we try to hide our feelings from ourselves and others. This creates many problems. First, we miss opportunities to deal with infuriating situations *before* they reach the boiling point. Second, we are so uncomfortable when other people are angry or enraged that we duck out or find a place to hide. In fact, women say that anger and rage in others are the top two emotions that make them uncomfortable.

EMOTIONS IN OTHERS THAT MAKE US MOST UNCOMFORTABLE

%	Anger	Rage	Despair	Jealousy
45				
	x			
40	x			
	x			
35	x			
	x	x		
30	x	x		
	x	x		
25	x	x		
	x y	x y	x	y
20	x y	x y	x	y
	x y	x y	x	y
15	x y	x y	x	y
	x y	x y	x	y
10	x y	x y	x	y
	x y	x y	x	y
5	x y	x y	x	y
	x y	x y	x	y

x = women   y = men

We dislike rage, so we fear confronting it. We also fear the physical harm that can come from rage. Listen to Joanna's story:

> It was my senior prom night. I really hadn't discussed with my parents what my plans were because I didn't *know* what they were. After the prom we went to a party, and after the party we all went down to the beach. Everyone fell asleep. Nothing happened. Around six someone woke us all up and we went home.
>
> My mother was waiting and my father was already gone. Mom told me he was so enraged that he was afraid of what he would do if he saw me face-to-face. Then I got scared and left too. By dinner, Dad and I were both back, but shaken.

Joanna's father ran from his rage. So did Joanna. Some of us try to hide it instead. The problem with hidden rage is that angry people usually turn out to be hiding their feelings from themselves more successfully than from anyone else. Everyone knows that something is wrong, but nobody can guess what it is or take steps to change it. The unrecognized rage may even find expression in distorted and inefficient forms, often appearing as depression, projection, or displacement and making communication and resolution even more difficult.

Depression protects us against acting on our rage by persuading us that nothing matters.

> Hank's officemate was promoted, turning his good friend into his boss—and a tough one at that. Though he had to admire his friend's performance, Hank soon found himself fatigued, disinterested in dating and his weekly tennis game. He spent a month of nights snacking in front of the television set and crawling off to bed exhausted. He finally recognized how furious he was about the promotion decision that had left him behind and simultaneously complicated a relationship he had valued.

In fact, depression only postpones the rage and turns it inward. We may think we are protecting others from our anger, but we are more often depriving them of our positive passions in the process.

Projection protects us against rage by making us so aware of other people's anger that we feel docile by comparison. When we are projecting, we believe that *they* are always starting arguments with *us*. That way we get to have our fights without admitting our role.

> Judy had had a hard day at the office. The highway was jammed, the supermarket was crowded, and the kids' bikes were blocking the driveway when she got home. She wanted to scream but felt guilty at the mere thought of taking out her irritability on her family. She composed herself, walked into the house—and bristled when she saw her husband's face. "I know that look," she snapped. "You're wondering why dinner's late. Well, fix your own dinner. I'm tired of being taken advantage of around here!" A bewildered husband watched Judy go into the bedroom and slam the door.

If Judy had been aware of her projection, we would call it rationalization or manipulation. But it was not until the next day that Judy could see what had happened.

Displacement occurs when we direct fury that belongs to one object to another—usually a neutral object, an innocent person, or even ourselves.

> It was four o'clock and Mona's doctor still had not called. She had phoned the office twice for her test results, and each time the nurse promised to call back. Now the office was closed. If she called the emergency number, the doctor would never respect her again. If she yelled at the nurse tomorrow, she would probably never get her results at all. So she yelled at her son instead. Then she threw the cat out of the house—it was shedding on the sofa *again!*—and fumed when she cut herself cleaning carrots for dinner.

Had Mona's son and Mona's cat done anything to deserve such treatment? Their only crime was being in the way of her displacement. Even her finger got in her way. When you find that little things are getting a big rage response from you, ask yourself whether your rage might need redirection.

Rage can also be a sign of underlying, relatively serious disease. Along with experiencing vision and hearing disorders, speech deficits, excessive physical energy, coordination problems, impulsivity, and intense and frequent frustration, children who are hyperactive often explode into rages. In some people, hyperactivity extends into adulthood. For women, PMS (premenstrual syndrome) may lower the threshold for rage by increasing irritability and causing an array of physical symptoms. One cause may be a change in the threshold for rage as the ratio of estrogen, the female sex hormone, to progesterone, the tranquility hormone, shifts. Another may be a drop in beta-endorphin, the happiness hormone. To limit PMS-related irritability: avoid caffeine, and get some high-quality aerobic exercise every day. If your PMS reactions are interfering with your daily life, see your gynecologist for information on the latest interventions and treatments.

Rage Management

Can we do better with our rage? Absolutely. The next time you are enraged, try the suggestion that fits best.

• *Wait.* Count to ten, then ten again. This old-fashioned, highly effective gimmick will give you time to formulate an *active* rather than a *reactive* response. Actively focus on the real cause of your rage instead of reacting at random to its effect on you. This will help prevent your anger from escalating and your rage from returning repeatedly. It will also help you regain a sense of control just when you are most afraid of being out of control.

• *Communicate.* Unlike other species, which have fangs, beaks, and poisons for protection, we have words available for negotiation. Use them. Neither lashing out physically nor freezing verbally will accomplish as much as communication. Physical violence only leads to physical violence. Verbal withdrawal leads into one-sided, imaginary conversations with no end. If you are alone, write out your feelings. Letters can be reviewed objectively and saved or discarded more easily than relationships.

• *Activate.* Rage produces adrenaline that needs to be used, so if you are faced with an enraging situation over which you have no real or immediate control, substitute a constructive activity for a destructive rage response. You can use up your extra adrenaline by exercising, dancing, cleaning closets, painting walls, playing tennis, or even moving furniture until you are tired enough to rest and relax.

Perhaps most important is to keep remembering that like other intense emotions, *rage passes.* If it returns so often you have the feeling it never leaves, examine your inner and outer life carefully. Are your life circumstances really so outrageous? Call on friends, relatives, and social agencies to help you change them.

If your inner life is the problem, you may have formed a rage habit. Some of us have never given up old rage because we would feel too vulnerable without our armor of anger. Professional counseling can help.

Above all, bear in mind that with rage, as with other emotions, what we expect is often what we get. We create self-fulfilling prophecies. Let's make them prophecies of wonder, hope, love, and joy rather than rage.

GUILT:
The Voice of Blame and Shame

6

uilt probably runs on a droplet of a neurotransmitter, which is lighter than a feather. It is processed through the brain, which weighs about three pounds. Why then does guilt feel so heavy when it sits on the heart? It is hard to laugh or enjoy anything for very long. You suffer your guilt over and over and spend your time searching for ways to unload it or do penance. You perspire, your appetite dwindles, your stomach knots, your digestion is upset, and you have no energy.

How guilt-prone are you? How do you respond to these statements?

1. I take pride in accomplishments.
2. I delay gratification and undertake difficult or unpopular tasks.
3. I'm concerned about the effects of my actions on others.
4. I feel constrained by obligations.
5. I feel inadequate.
6. I feel guilty for not living up to standards or for letting someone down.

If you said yes to the first two statements, you are able to operate with a minimal guilt response. If you said yes to statements 3 and

4, you are more guilt-prone. If you said yes to statements 5 and 6, you are probably suffering from guilt right now! Do not be alarmed if you are. Most people are selectively guilt-prone and would have answered yes to most of these statements.

How Guilt Gets Started

When you were a child, guilt probably did not last as long as it does now, because it was usually followed quickly by either punishment or forgiveness. Remember those first feelings? Up to about age two, you did not care what the world wanted you to do, and that was fine with the people around you—after all, you were just a baby and still learning. In your third year, though, you were beginning to tell wrong from right. That is when your capacity for feeling shamed and publicly embarrassed develops. But real guilt comes a bit later. Sigmund Freud, Jean Piaget, and Laurence Kohlberg studied child development, and their theories all agree that the capacity for real guilt—an internalized sense of what is bad and good—does not develop until the end of the preschool period. By age three and a half to four and a half, the child knows "what is naughty and what is nice." When they do something "naughty," something they "should not do," and feel guilty, we say children have developed a conscience. A mother tells the story of her little girl's growing awareness of conscience:

> When Mary Jane was two years old, she ate some candy before dinner. I explained why it is better not to eat so close to mealtime, but of course she did not understand—she was too little. When she was five years old, she did the same thing and I explained why again, this time with anger from me and a kicking temper tantrum from her. An hour later I went into my bedroom and there was a note on the dressing table. It said, I M S I K. I rushed out to find Mary Jane and asked her if she was sick. "No," she said, sur-

prised. "Then what is this here on this piece of paper?" I asked gently. She said, "I am sorry I kicked."

When children do not do something they "should do," when they are not "nice," and feel guilty, we say they have developed ego ideal.

Ray came home from kindergarten with a sad look on his face. He did not eat well that evening or sleep well that night. By morning he was ready to talk about it. A new boy who looked strange had come to class last week, Ray explained. He had a funny lip and spoke funny and was very small. Ray stopped talking and his eyes filled with tears. "Are you crying because you feel bad for this boy?" his mother asked. "No!" he protested too loudly. "It's because I didn't stop Steve from beating him up!"

As we mature, it is our ego ideal that will cause us more guilt than our conscience. We will have less time and inclination to be "bad," but more and more situations in which we feel we have not been "good enough." We must be wary of the "shoulds." Sometimes they help us grow, but often, as adults, our expectations for ourselves and our guilt multiply endlessly.

If you are tempted to blame your parents for programming you for excessive guilt, your feelings might be well placed. Although we are born with a *capacity* for guilt, we learn what to feel guilty *about,* what is good and what is bad, from our families. The degree of guilt we feel as adults may relate to the degree of guilt we were taught to feel as children.

Some explanations of guilt stray from the issue of simple right and wrong. Researchers have shown that children reared by depressed mothers show more guilt than children whose mothers were normal. When researchers read a story involving emotional conflict to children with and without depressed mothers, the children of the depressed mothers were more sensitive to others' problems and tended to blame the children in the story for the conflict, to see the children as guilty. They showed this evidence of guilt at an earlier age than the children whose mothers were not depressed. And at the age when normal remorse for bad behavior was developing in others, these children of depressed mothers often expressed unusual forms of guilt, such as hypersensitivity to others' feelings, bizarre behavior, and even violence.

Although the capacity for guilt is inborn, and our environment reinforces very early what to feel guilty about, this does not mean our guilt is beyond control as we grow older. We can understand it and change it.

Guilt's Many Guises

In my survey of emotions, guilt did not turn up as a frequent male emotion. Only 1.6 percent of men said it was their most common emotion. But 14.2 percent of the women in the survey said it was their *most common emotion*. In addition, women report feeling a little more uncomfortable with guilt than men do, and they say they hide it more:

MEN, WOMEN, AND GUILT

20			x		x	
			x		x	
15	x		x	y	x	
	x		x	y	x	
10	x		x	y	x	y
	x		x	y	x	y
5	x		x	y	x	y
	x	y	x	y	x	y

% who said guilt was their most common emotion	% who find guilt the most uncomfortable emotion	% who hide their guilt

x = women y = men

People Guilt

More information comes from the questionnaire sentence-completion item about guilt. The most common source of guilt, it seems, is other people. Among the women's reasons for guilt were guilt about a daughter, a divorce, and mistreating a sibling when young. Others worried about not meeting everyone's needs. We allow other people to be the measure of the bad things we have done and the good things we have not done. Our mothers, fathers, sisters, brothers, and children make us feel guilty; so do our boyfriends, girlfriends, and other people whose opinions we respect.

Kary's mother lived alone, and maybe that is why Christmas was such a critical time for her. She asked Kary to bring her husband and two girls over for Christmas day festivities, and Kary agreed. But then Mom mentioned the Christmas Eve church service, and that would mean an overnight for Kary and her family, since her mother lived about seventy miles away. Kary reluctantly agreed. *Then* Mom called Kary back to tell her that Aunt Sylvia would be coming by two days after Christmas, and to invite Kary to come by again *that* day for coffee. Come by! After a seventy-mile drive! Kary said it would be too much. Her mother's voice suddenly sounded lower, and her tone changed—she was hurt. And Kary? Kary felt guilty for being so unwilling to drive to her mother's house twice at this important time of year.

Almost anybody who is aware of other people's feelings lives with some guilt. We simply cannot do everything that everyone else would like. We feel inadequate because if our standard is perfection, we are inadequate. To counter such feelings, we need to remind ourselves of what is possible to do and be realistic about the rest.

When you feel guilty, ask yourself: What is the source of the guilt? Have I been bad or just not good enough? Kary's mother's feelings of isolation may have been real, but Kary can only do what she can do. Instead of letting her mother's disappointment get to her and wasting time on guilt, she could have looked for some solutions—perhaps more visits to her mother at other times of the year, or a sympathetic negotiation with her mother's sister for a more timely visit. Most of us need practice saying no without defensiveness, resentment, indignation—without guilt. We need to say no with kindness, sympathy, or firmness instead. Practice makes perfect, and the guilt response is a hard habit to break. So start today, just say no!

Sexual Guilt

The society we live in sends us many messages about the female sex.

- Be sexy but not too sexual.
- Be interesting but not too interested.
- Be assertive but not sexually aggressive.
- Be liberated, but protect yourself from gossip, from disease, and from unwanted pregnancy.

We grow up hearing these messages, and eventually we internalize them. That is, we change them from external (something imposed upon us) to internal (something we impose upon ourselves). The sound of others' voices becomes our own small voice inside our head. Listen to the sound of two voices. At first they seem almost the same, but read carefully and you will see a difference:

> Jill was twenty-two and living at home when she met Ron at a wedding. They were instantly attracted—he was a little wild, just the sort of guy her parents would not like at all, and that was exciting. Jill and Ron had sex at the beach, in the back of the car, on the floor in his apartment.
>
> One night Ron suggested they do it in the backyard of the house where Jill was living—her parents' backyard, that is. Jill lay down a blanket, and she and Ron moved quickly through the preliminaries. But instead of feeling hot, she was beginning to feel a little chilly. When he tried to make love, she went cold.

Compare Jill's story to Lisa's:

Lisa was twenty-two and had always told herself she would not
do one-night stands, but this guy was so *sexy*, his blue blazer fit so
well. Just by a look and a touch, he conveyed the promise of
knowledgeable, lose-yourself lovemaking; Lisa had had enough
wine to make her totally receptive. "Go ahead," whispered Lisa's
friend Natalie, who had invited Jim to the party and knew him
well. And their night together was indeed spectacular.

Their second date did not go so smoothly. Though Jim took her
to a very nice brunch, with free refills on the Bloody Marys, Lisa
felt he was just waiting to loosen her up and get her back to his
apartment. She realized she did not know Jim well at all beyond
the fact that he was something of an operator, and she found that
the sexiness she had felt by night had turned to shame in the
daylight. So she took his hand and said, "Jim—I'm sorry. I'm just
not feeling right about this."

What was the difference between Jill's guilt and Lisa's? For Jill,
the source of guilt was her parents. She knew her parents did not
approve of premarital sex, and she suspected they would not be too
thrilled about backyard sex, either. Even though she was growing
up, she still felt a desire to please them, or at least to avoid awak-
ening their wrath.

Lisa, the party girl, was on her own, in full control of her own sex
life. The little voice she heard in her head that made her feel uneasy
with Jim was her own voice, and it was telling her that this kind of
sex was simply not right for her. It may not even have been guilt
that stopped her from going to bed with Jim a second time. It may
have been a more basic idea about her own self-protection. Lisa
thought that a person as free with sex as Jim would *probably* not
make a faithful partner, and she knew that when she slept with
someone, her feelings often deepened even if she did not want
them to. So she decided not to take the chance.

As we all grow older, we gather sexual experience. Sometimes
we carry into maturity and marriage the rigid rules our parents may

have designed to help us navigate through adolescence and young adulthood. In fact, at one time, marriage was a psychic shock: One moment we were supposed to be the virgin our father was giving away to another man, and the next minute we were supposed to be the fulfillment of that man's most sensual dreams. One woman I know told me that even after she was *married*, she did not feel comfortable sleeping in the same bed with a man in her parents' home—and she was married on her thirtieth birthday! She was old enough to make her own rules about her life. Guilt runs deep.

Subconscious Conflicts

Life is full of mixed feelings, and mixed feelings are hard to act on. So we often bury the inconvenient feelings. But they do not stay buried for long. Sometimes, when it really seems we are feeling guilty for no reason at all, the problem is often a conflict.

"Mom, I've been feeling real guilty, and I don't know why," Patty said during one of her weekly phone conversations with her mother. She knew she wanted to visit her parents more, but she really had been terribly busy with her job, and her mother understood. Patty was drowning in a painful sense of guilt that she could not define. She was helpless to do anything about it and felt overwhelmed.

Because Patty loved her parents, it is possible that growing up and away from them was as painful as it was exciting for her. This was her conflict. She wanted to remain their little girl but be an adult too. So she kept herself very busy and even did a few things they would not have approved of, hurrying the separation process along at full speed. If Patty had identified how natural it is to have mixed feelings about launching herself into a new life and leaving her parents behind, she could have spared herself some guilt and discomfort.

Men have similar conflicts or mixed feelings. For example, a young man may feel guilty when he thinks about not meeting his father's expectations—and equally guilty when he thinks about exceeding them and overshadowing his father. Or he may have mixed feelings about a new baby: He loves the baby but he resents that he suddenly is no longer his wife's one-and-only object of attention. He then feels guilty about his resentment and tries to bury it.

Life is full of mixed feelings! To live with less guilt, we have to learn to live with more mixed feelings. Like mixed blessings, they are a fact of life.

Guilt That Will Not Go

Sometimes people make mistakes. We accidentally spill hot water on a child or pet, hurt or kill with our cars, have babies out of wedlock and then give them away, make decisions that cause people pain. Afterward, we feel guilt with a vengeance, and it is very hard to eradicate. Identifying the source is no help at all; you know the source, and it is painful. One man tells his story:

> It's more than ten years since Deborah died, but my wife and I still think of her every day. We still wonder if she'd be alive if we'd done things differently.
>
> We were young, just married, and united in our mistrust of the establishment. I guess you could call us children of the sixties. So when she got pregnant, we agreed that the birth would be at home, with everything as natural as possible. Her due date passed, and two weeks later our obstetrician advised us to induce labor in the hospital. We refused. Finally, a week later, Deborah was born at home. She had heart and breathing problems caused by the fact that the placenta had begun to disintegrate. The doctor and mid-wife tried to save her, but twenty minutes after she was born, she

was dead. My wife and I held her and just cried and cried and cried.

Today I wonder how we could have been so . . . I want to say stupid, but I've come far enough along in forgiving us that I know we were doing what we believed. But guilt can't bring her back.

How much can we expect from ourselves? Can we expect perfection? Of course not, we say. But then we return to our perfectionism. We must not make mistakes, we tell ourselves. We must try to do everything right the first time. We try to make our work flawless, our homes spotless. Even our spouses and children become extensions of ourselves. So when our work, our homes, our families, and our own actions disappoint us, we feel guilty, guilty, guilty about falling so short.

It is not noble to want perfection; it is cruel. It makes others feel inadequate and undermines our own self-esteem. It is self-imposed mental cruelty. The real world is full of imperfections, and the real world is the one we live in. We could spend the rest of our lives feeling guilty—or we can accept our imperfections as part of what is real.

Guiltbusters

There are many ways to deal with guilt, and you have control over all of them.

The first step is usually identifying the source of the guilt. Is it in the past or present? Is someone else making you feel guilty or are you doing it to yourself? You will need this information for several of the following actions you can take.

Apologize If the source of your guilt is something you said or did to another person, try saying you are sorry. You may be surprised to find that the thing you feel guilty about has already been forgiven and forgotten. Your apology is not accepted? At least you tried.

Make amends   If apology is out of the question, perhaps you can still find a way to set things right. You can replace something you broke, redo something you did poorly, return something you stole. Our legal system gives guilty people a chance to pay for their crimes—ex-drug users speak to young addicts, graffitists wipe away their artwork and repaint—shouldn't our own personal ethic system do the same?

Prescribe yourself a restitution   But be sure it fits the "crime": Flagellating yourself just makes more pain and does not contribute anything to the good of the world. So go for logical consequences. Were you rude to a friend? Apologize, and then donate an hour's time to volunteer work in her name.

Get outside help   If your guilt is interfering with your daily life, psychotherapy may help. Its mission is to deal with the prominence of inappropriate guilt in your life. If you feel uncomfortable talking about guilt with a psychotherapist, you should know that he or she will not be surprised by what you have to say. Guilt is common. A psychotherapist will help you work through it and arrive at forgiveness or acceptance.

Set a time limit, and then dismiss the guilt   If there is no way for you to apologize, no amends you can make, no penance you can do, no therapist who can help you, and you cannot find forgiveness, then set a limit on your guilt and prepare to dismiss it. It is not doing you any good. First spend one solid hour feeling guilty and thinking about nothing else. Then be finished with your guilt. If symbols are meaningful to you, buy a helium balloon and imagine it is your guilt. Then go outside and release your balloon into the air, up and away.

Pray or meditate   If you are religious, ask God to forgive you. As you pray or meditate, you may find that ideas for action you can take may come to you as well.

Finally, forgive yourself   Everybody makes mistakes. Even if everyone around you forgives you, you will still have to forgive yourself. Do!

ENHANCING YOUR POSITIVE PASSIONS

Now is the time for those wonderful passions that have always seemed so fleeting. Our favorite positive emotions, according to my Passions Survey, are contentment, hope, joy, and love, in that order. A majority of respondents say you already have quantities of these peak emotions in your life. Only one fourth of respondents say the negative emotions—anxiety, fear, despair, and guilt—are your most frequent feelings.

You say you feel good feelings. And yet you say you yearn for more. Your wish can be granted! Positive passions are not just lucky moments. They can be created again and again if you know how.

The Four Fears

The first step to putting more of the positive passions in your life is to remove barriers that block them. If you are having trouble feeling positive passions, you may be experiencing one or more of the four fears.

Fear of the price tag   Positive emotions do not cost. There may be no free breakfast, lunch, or dinner, but you can satisfy your appetite for joy, love, hope, and awe without paying a penny. Positive passions are already part of you. They are your birthright. If you are paying to feel something, you are wasting money or whatever else you are investing. You do not have to buy your emotions.

Similarly, if you *hold in* your emotions because you think you may have to pay *later*, you are wasting your energy. No evil eye is watching you and keeping a tab on how much hope you will have today so that you can be "billed" in despair tomorrow. Good feelings are a gift that life gives us in quantity. You cannot physically sustain peak emotions for long periods of time—your body and mind would become exhausted—but you can definitely enhance the emotions you prefer or feel them more often.

Fear of the unknown   Some people say that love is always new: Each time we fall in love, it is as if we have never felt it before. *I never knew it could be like this . . . you're the first person I've ever really loved.* We murmur such things about other good feelings, too: *I've never seen such a beautiful place before . . . If only I could win this prize . . .* All strong emotions are new.

To many of us, the novelty is frightening, even when the emotion is powerfully positive. The emotion is as big as the ocean and we are in a small boat. Then our boat is lifted high on the crest of a wave. Terror! We reach for the life preserver.

Or it can feel pleasurable. Waves rise and then they return to sea level; meanwhile, on top of the wave, we have had an extraordinary view. And there is truth in the analogy with the small boat. We have our individuality, we have a certain amount of control, but in a universe full of natural forces, in a world alive with many things that we and billions of people like us do not understand, we *are* small. It is not bad to recognize that. It is a reason to rejoice in the forces within us, to ride the forces that move us. Poets, philosophers, and lovers have spent lakefuls of ink lingering over love, beauty, nature, and good, and their sentiments tell us we are not alone.

Practice can keep the good feelings coming. Whether it is cooking Thai, telling a lie, or feeling an emotion, it is always easier the second time. You already know that if you practice despair, rage, fear, or guilt, they will, unfortunately, come more easily to you. So do joy, hope, awe, and other positive passions. Practice these instead.

Once the sensations of good feelings become familiar, you will find that you will resist them less and slip into them more naturally. It is a principle called operant conditioning: You try something, you get a reward, you are more likely to try the same thing again. Since the positive emotions are their own reward, you will quickly learn to be more open to them in the future. If you fear they will dissolve and leave you feeling bereft, do not forget that you can create more.

Fear of seeming overglad   In the classic movie *Pollyanna*, a neglected girl learns to find happiness. It is an uplifting story, too uplifting for some people. As adults, we fear being overpositive or taking excessive pleasure in a world where misfortune and tragedy are so obvious. If this is your worry, consider that dragging a heavy burden with you all the time will not make life better for anyone. Offering others and yourself a rest from negative feelings and a glimpse of positive ones could give someone the courage to go on. Positive emotions can generate ideas and action.

Fear of punishment   One of the good things about being an adult is that we can take care of ourselves. Ever since we were teenagers, and possibly before, we looked ahead to the day when we could set our own bedtime, spend money as we wished, and get away from people who told us what to do. But we carry those people's punishing voices in our heads all our lives. You can probably remember something specific that someone said to you when you were younger.

Eight-year-old Lilli knew that her mother acted strangely sometimes, but Lilli was too young to understand just what alcoholism meant. So when she came home from school and found a note from her mother on her pillow, she believed every word of it and blamed herself:

Lilli is   SELFISH
         ANNOYING
         UGLY
         FAT
         BAD
         BORING
I wish you had never been born

Lilli read the note, cried into her pillow, and promised herself she would do better. Twenty years later, Lilli understands that her mother's alcoholism was an illness and tells about the note as an example of the horrors of her childhood—but she still remembers every word.

If you do not feel entitled to joy, love, hope, awe, or any of the many wonderful emotions people feel, maybe someone long ago made you believe you did not deserve them and punished you when you tried to have them. Teachers, parents, peers, and other people whose opinions we care about can give us this message. Even if you do not recall exactly how people manipulated you, you may have internalized it—made it a part of yourself—until that way of thinking became your own. As an adult, you may have to work to undo damage done in your past. Here is a start: Recognize that you have a right to be here even if you were an unwanted child. You can be beautiful even if someone said you were not. You are lovable and can love even if you do not know it yet.

Joy, love, hope, and awe are for you. We are born entitled to experience our capacities for positive peak emotions—so look for opportunities. Do not wait for someone to come up and offer them to you. That rarely happens. You have to find them for yourself.

Chemical Passions and Drug Vacations

Many of us take wrong turns in our pursuit of positive passions.

When we feel sad, we feel like we are standing on one side of the Grand Canyon and happiness is far on the other side. A chasm separates us from where we would like to be. We see no obvious way across. Is this a time when you have considered chemical bridges? These can seem to offer a way across, but the toll is astronomical. The chemical bridges which seem to promise a shortcut to passions, are stimulants, tranquilizers, and recreational drugs.

Stimulants are common in our culture. We are busy; we are tired; we are feeling a little down. We use up our supply of energy and so we start running on adrenaline. What we really need, before the adrenaline has poured out and the blood sugar has burned up, is rest and time to generate more real energy. What we take instead are stimulants: caffeine, nicotine, amphetamines, and cocaine. The feeling is familiar. With both endogenous stimulants and artificial ones, our heart pumps more quickly, our respiration is increased, our mind seems sharper, our appetite is temporarily suppressed. Depression is counteracted, delayed, or disguised temporarily. For the moment there is no need to feel we are losing life's battle by slowing down or running out of ammunition. For the moment we are feeling important, useful, and competent. For the moment, with an artificial stimulant to help, we feel very much alive and ready for anything. Louise tells a story of housewife life:

> I feel more tired in a nice house with two nice kids than I did working an eleven-hour day in a crummy office. Maybe because at the office someone sees what you do and gives a little support.

At home you've got to get on the kids' coats, boots, hats, scarves, and gloves by 8:15 and have everyone to school by 8:30 or the teacher marks your kids late. Then you come home to an empty house. Nobody says thank you. You get tired and lonely. That diet pill is like a reward for the stuff you've done so far, and it gives you the strength and energy to do another couple hours' work in the house before everyone gets home.

All of the artificial stimulants share some effects on the central nervous system, which includes the brain and the spinal cord. In general, they kick us into action by:

- stimulating the cerebral cortex, which handles thought processes and is the center of energy, action, and optimism;
- stimulating the medulla, which regulates heart rate, respiration, and coordination, increasing cell metabolism;
- signaling the release of adrenaline, which stimulates the nerve cells that trigger our action muscles.

Caffeine is one of a group of chemical compounds called xanthines. Caffeine temporarily stimulates the central nervous system, boosting metabolism, increasing cardiac activity, and releasing sugar into the bloodstream. The effects include energy, alertness, and greater endurance for an hour or two. Caffeine boosts simple motor activity, like chores and routines, but interferes with complex activities like tiny repairs or calligraphy. Caffeine also arouses your sensory neurons, making dessert or a cigarette more flavorful. Finally, caffeine is a mild diuretic.

But a dangerous drug? It can be. Depending upon your weight and tolerance, at the seven- to ten-cup-a-day level you stop feeling the good effects and start feeling some bad ones—insomnia, stomach upset, nervousness. Keep increasing your intake, and you may encounter two other symptoms of caffeinism—delirium and sensory disturbances.

Besides giving a harried man or woman the chance to sit down for a moment, *cigarettes* carry an effective chemical, nicotine, to the brain within seconds of the first inhale. There, it lifts mood, reduces appetite, and fights fatigue.

A lifetime of cigarette smoking has other effects you have no doubt already heard about: cancers of the mouth, throat, larynx, esophagus, lungs, bladder, kidney, and pancreas; lung disease, heart disease; and aggravation of peptic ulcers, high blood pressure, and sleep disorders. A woman smoker who uses oral contraceptives probably has a higher chance of cardiovascular problems than the woman on other types of birth control. Smoking contributes to Buerger's disease, in which the blood vessels constrict and cause gangrene. In pregnant women, the nicotine and other chemicals circulate through the baby's body, later contributing to fetal problems such as low birth weight, short stature in the child, and impaired reading ability. Pregnant smokers also have a higher risk of spontaneous abortion and stillbirth.

Amphetamines, also known as speed, produce intense alertness and false confidence. A woman on amphetamines who a few minutes earlier was too tired to decide what video to have delivered is now ready to mail out a few résumés and start writing an article for the professional journal in her career field. Amphetamines make users temporarily talkative, excited, and restless. They feel like they have endless energy and boundless insight. The huge energy rush makes amphetamines especially popular with students, performers, athletes, and truck drivers. Drug-enforcement officials are concerned that a synthetic, smokable form of amphetamine called crystal methamphetamine (or ice) will be the drug blight of the 1990s. Working mothers who take crystal meth have said it makes them feel like Superwoman but act like a narrowly focused compulsive. One woman tells of cleaning her kitchen floor for hours with a toothbrush.

It is easy to become psychologically dependent on amphetamines. You may even enjoy some of the side effects: less appetite and weight loss are two. You may not enjoy the others, though: a dry mouth and nose, a higher body temperature, a more rapid heartbeat, higher blood pressure, and faster breathing. A regular user may find that one pill does not do what it once did, because tolerance builds rapidly. Soon too many uppers cause an irregular heartbeat, restlessness, dizziness, anxiety, and aggressive or violent behavior. Then amphetamines create chronic fatigue; a loss of appetite that results in malnutrition, depression, or suicidal thoughts; and even paranoia and other psychoses or breaks with reality.

Cocaine and its derivative, crack, are stimulants in the same class of drugs as amphetamines. They also act on the central nervous system, raising the breathing rate, heart rate, blood pressure, and body temperature. Like all the other stimulants, they wake you up and shut your appetite down. At the peak of the high, which comes on quickly because cocaine is absorbed through the nasal mucous membranes, a user feels an all-surpassing well-being and warmth toward other people and a sense of great personal power and intelligence. But it is a very short-lived effect, and the next "hit" must follow quickly or you are feeling its loss. A single guy who uses the name Judd knows about that:

> The first time I went into a Los Angeles disco, it was so cavernous, there were so many bodies . . . I held on to my girlfriend's hand. We were overwhelmed, two babes in toyland. Then on our way upstairs a guy invited us into the men's room. We knew why and went in. When we came out we felt much better. The DJ was playing a record about friends. We would dance three beats, and on the fourth everyone on the floor would say, "Friends."
>
> Everyone was smiling, and the mood was golden. I'll never forget what it was like to be friends with so many people at one time.
>
> Then the music began to grate on me and I became annoyed that it was too slow. Everyone around me was looking at me, I thought, and I yelled at them to stop staring.

Like amphetamines, cocaine creates a strong psychological dependence. Users often have trouble getting along without its pleasant high and take dose after dose of this expensive drug. Common

long-term effects of regular cocaine use include restlessness, paranoia, sleeplessness, hallucinations, and delusions, including formi-
cation, the sensation that insects or snakes are crawling under
your skin. A chronic user can also burn out the mucous membranes lining her nose. We know now too, after the heart-attack
deaths of many healthy young athletes, that taking this central
nervous system stimulant is playing cardiac roulette. Cocaine creates an artificial emotional peak that can leave us paranoid,
broke, or dead.

If the downs of our lives lead some of us to stimulants, then what
do we do when we are too up—too nervous, too hyper—to feel
comfortable? Many people turn to relaxants and tranquilizers.
Sometimes stimulant users turn to these downer drugs when their
uppers have taken them too high.

Alcohol enters our bloodstream quickly and is in the brain within
a few minutes. The most common reasons we use this cheap, powerful sedative-hypnotic drug are to release inhibitions, to relax, to
mask loneliness, low self-esteem, sex-role conflicts, and to reduce
our fear of failure. We tell ourselves that we are putting life back in
our life by drinking as we become disinhibited. The impulses we
find unacceptable when we are sober begin to show. If we are
reluctant to show weakness, alcohol may let us cry. If we inhibit all
hostility when we are dry, we may fight and even brutalize when
we are drinking. If sex is taboo when we are in control, the lamp-
shade may be on our head and passion in our breast when we are
drunk. The intoxicated sob-sister, wife abuser, or promiscuous flirt
may come out when we are under the influence. Alcohol has been
the false muse of many a passionate writer and artist.

The ethanol in alcohol literally numbs the central nervous system, first depressing memory, intelligence, caution, and self-
control. In addition to making you forget errands, miss meetings,
spend too much at the department store, have a car accident, and/or
offend people with your frankness, alcohol also starts to tamper
with the senses, coordination, and balance.

Frances has a hard time finding people to drink with. In this health-conscious age, nobody seems to do it much anymore. She tries not to drink alone, but she creates as many drinking occasions as possible: lunch parties, book club parties, and matinee parties with friends who enjoy getting a little tipsy with her. One day after a well-lubricated restaurant lunch in the city, Frances fell in the street and hurt her knees. When her family asked about her bruises, she told them she had slipped on the steps of the house. It was the first of many lies Frances would tell to conceal how much she was drinking.

If you drink enough alcohol, it affects the vital life centers by totally relaxing the muscles that control breathing. A drinker rarely gets that far without vomiting or going into a coma first, which prevents the fatal drink. But if heavy drinking goes on for years, the liver becomes inefficient or blocked (cirrhosis). The drinker has an increased risk of mouth, esophagus, stomach, and breast cancer. The alcohol may hit the nervous system, triggering amnesia, disorientation, loss of short-term memory, hallucinations, emotional disturbances, loss of muscle control, double vision, and, possibly, depression, aggression, antisocial behavior, and anxiety—exactly the states of mind the drinker had hoped to escape.

The doctor who agrees that you must sleep and eat and work although you are going through a short-term, high-anxiety reaction to a real-life crisis will probably prescribe a minor *tranquilizer*. These drugs are meant to help quiet the buzz in your head, relax you, and enable you to think more clearly about the problems at hand with less of the drowsiness some over-the-counter calmers bring. If you cannot sleep, the doctor may prescribe *barbiturates*. In small doses, these sedative-hypnotics can induce relaxation and even mild euphoria. In larger doses of both tranquilizers and sleeping pills—which the regular user eventually needs—the effects can be slurred speech, slowed reflexes, trouble walking, mental confusion, or drowsiness. If the dose is high enough, the consequences can be unconsciousness or death, as the drugs relax the muscles that control circulation and breathing to the point that they stop working altogether. The barbiturate addict who survives for the long term may find herself experiencing highly unwelcome anxiety, insomnia, paranoia, and suicidal depression.

Barbiturates and tranquilizers are sometimes called alcohol in pills because they depress the central nervous system in a similar way. Like alcohol, barbiturates and some benzodiazepines (especially Valium—the one the Rolling Stones called "mother's little helper") are hard to give up. The user deprived of her fix may get the shakes, also known as delirium tremens, or DTs; have a rapid pulse; feel weak, anxious, and restless; hallucinate; or even go into life-threatening convulsions.

People reach for *psychedelic drugs* such as marijuana (pot) and LSD (acid) for their effect on the senses. What you see, taste, feel, smell, and hear is altered or heightened. For a few hours the world is utterly fascinating, and you feel like you can laugh freely and deeply. With marijuana, food becomes a wonderful adventure. With LSD, sensory crossovers may create stunning hallucinogenic effects: music has colors, inanimate objects that breathe.

The physical side effects of even occasional marijuana use are: increased heart rate, sleepiness, altered depth perception, muscular weakness, and delayed reaction time. The effects of LSD and related drugs such as peyote and mescaline mimic the flight and fight syndrome: the pupils of the eyes dilate and blood pressure, heart rate, and body temperature increase.

Although these drugs are usually nonlethal except for suicide or a drug related accident, their use is no free trip. With both marijuana and LSD, there is always the risk of a bad psychological trip: Paranoia is common with both, and the distortion of reality can lead you to misjudge heights or the speed of your car. Suggestibility, anxiety, confusion, restlessness, anger, tears, fears, decreased concentration, difficulty in communicating—these side effects are unwelcome and can be tragic if they overwhelm the ability to cope.

Although psychedelic drugs are considered nonaddictive because there are no physical withdrawal symptoms, they can lead to psychological dependence. Long-term smoking of marijuana contributes to memory problems, lung inflammation and, possibly, lung cancer. Marijuana smoke contains 50 percent more carcinogens (cancer-causing agents) than tobacco smoke. Some research suggests that a pregnant woman who smokes marijuana is more likely than a non-smoking pregnant woman to have a spontaneous abortion, stillbirth, or smaller than normal baby because all the psychedelic drugs freely cross the placenta to the fetus. Someone who spends an afternoon tripping on acid can have a surprise "flashback" of visual or sensory disturbances many years later because the drug may not be fully excreted and less than one-millionth of an ounce is needed to induce mind-altering effects. This is a high price to pay for a brief vacation, and all the troubles you left behind are waiting for you when you come home.

Sexual Pseudopassion

For most of us, sex is pleasurable. For a few of us, sex is an addiction. For most of us, sexual activity makes us feel loved and wanted. For a few of us, not having sex creates anxiety and tension. For anyone, arousal can last an hour or two. That is not enough for the addict. The sex addict pursues sex the way a drug addict pursues a fix. No matter what the cause of anxiety or stress, for them the answer is always sexual release.

Enough biochemical changes seem to take place in the sexually aroused brain to alter one's state of consciousness. Flooded with endorphins, norepinephrine, dopamine, serotonin, and phenylethylamine, the brain's pleasure center becomes exquisitely sensitized to visual, verbal, and touch cues. The need for sleep decreases, impulse control becomes challenged, and reality testing becomes wrecked. One feels optimistic in the face of all odds, and energized.

Why? Endorphins are morphinelike painkillers. Phenylethylamine can produce an amphetaminelike rush. Serotonin levels are associated with delusions and hallucinations. Norepinephrine provides bursts of energy, and dopamine counteracts depression.

Is there withdrawal discomfort from these natural endogenous "drugs"? Are these sexual antidepressants potentially addictive? In other words, can one lose a sense of control over sexual behavior? It seems to me that for some, the answer is, unfortunately, yes. Withdrawal from sexual arousal means that the adrenaline stops pouring into the bloodstream, heart rate slows again, and reality reenters. It is the nature of peak experiences that they cannot last. There is a limit to our physical capacity for arousal and our emotional capacity for suspending reality.

If the sexual behavior is satisfying and reality is a comfortable place to be, the story ends here. If the sex adds excitement where there is loneliness, revenge where there is anger, a feeling of defiance where there is dependency, or reassurance where there is low self-esteem, withdrawal will be more painful. The fast fix? More instant intimacy, more sex.

We are not talking about a simple lack of willpower, an abnormally high libido, or a masochistic rite of self-destruction. Although even those who suffer from compulsive sexual behavior try to explain their seeming insatiability in one of these three ways, they do not sufficiently deal with the data. If lack of willpower were the only factor, why would this lack be confined to sex? Those who are sexually compulsive would also be obese, cigarette smokers, alcohol abusers, gambling neurotics, and they are not. According to the research of my colleague at Mount Sinai School of Medicine in New York, Michael Quadland, Ph.D., most are highly educated, well functioning, and not significantly more neurotic than nonsexually compulsive controls. Nor do they have a higher sex drive. They have, research tells us, less choice and control over their sexual behavior and certainly less sense of satisfaction.

Nor can I settle for an explanation that rests on self-abuse as a primary motive. Although compulsive sexual behavior may indeed turn out to be destructive of relationships, job stability, or self-esteem, it is likely that this behavior started as an attempt to make something *better*, not worse. Sexual self-abuse can be understood as a failed attempt to block anxiety rather than a successful attempt to create frustration and desperation. Consider Barbara, who could be any one of the more than one thousand women who participated in my study of compulsive behavior for *Quick Fixes & Small Comforts*:

> Barbara could diet and work long hours. She felt good, no matter how bad the weather forecast was, when she had a lover. Every time she had sex with him, she felt flushed and expansive. But as soon as they separated, all the good feelings she had gained were immediately lost. She made more and more sexual demands on him, and soon her calls outnumbered his. She would fight to keep herself from dialing his number and would lose the fight every time. The more upset she became, the more she concluded that she needed him to feel better.

Since sexual arousal involves the body as well as the mind, it is easy to confuse agitation with anticipation. When Barbara was having an affair, she labeled her pounding heart and sweating palms as passion. Without a sexual focus, the same sensations felt like *anxiety*—and probably were! So she would search for lover after lover to explain and contain her anxiety. If we look at Barbara dynamically, she is confusing emotional tension with sexual tension. General free-floating anxiety became focused on a fear that sex would not be available. Once her "fix" was secured, Barbara's anxiety level dropped temporarily. Unfortunately, with every sexual encounter, her behavior was reinforced, since she felt better for the moment. The next time tension built, the temporary cure was even more obvious and compelling. And tension always builds.

For those who would say that I am too quick to see psychological dynamics around every sexual corner, let us see how compulsive sexual behavior differs from a robust, healthy sex drive:

- First, if the sexual behavior is compulsive, its anticipation is likely to be tinged with conflict, embarrassment, or shame rather than hopeful enthusiasm.
- Second, relief is brief.
- Third, pleasure is not followed by comfort or satisfaction. Instead, the hunger to fill up again on passion seems barely whetted.
- Fourth, guilt and regret create new tensions. Self-esteem and a sense of control drop even lower. Insecurity, loneliness, and frustration climb.

Unlike the natural rhythm and flow of an uninhibited libido, this kind of sexual dependency is *driven, ritualized,* and *repetitive.* Sexual contacts are not spontaneous acts of caring and sharing but are reported as the only highs of the day or night, and panic builds if this fix is not available. Because of mislearning or predispositions we do not yet understand, the sex drive becomes entwined with other states of tension and the drive for sexual release becomes constant.

Therapy groups like Sexaholics Anonymous can help identify a need we are frantically trying to ignore and help to substitute more effective and efficient strategies for meeting our needs. If you do not want outsiders to help, that may be a sign that your fear of dependency is misplaced.

Cults

Cults come in many guises. Some cults answer our need for love or our need to belong. Some promise a life of joy, and if our own joy fades a little as cult life becomes everyday life, we have a constant flow of new recruits whose joy is contagious. Some cults offer strict physical or spiritual discipline, which we may think is our road to the joy of accomplishment. In other words, if we want it, there is probably a cult offering it. And at first, it feels great:

Al did not feel particularly gifted in any area, certainly not in the careers toward which his father kept pushing him. He took various unsatisfying jobs as he searched for something he wanted to do.

One day in a shopping mall, a man approached Al with some literature about a religious group. He seemed so together, so secure in himself, that Al was interested. He invited Al to a party in the building outside of town where he and his friends lived. Al went—and never left. He did some handy work for the group and the group encouraged him to write his parents a note saying he was okay. Soon he was transferred to another group center farther away. A group leader now asked him to tell his parents he was attending teacher's college and request money, which he did. He married a group member, and the two of them set about making money, turning all their earnings over to the group.

Al was lucky: eventually he came to suspect that he had given up his identity and had not gotten anything back, so one day he bought himself a ticket home. Fortunately, the cult did not keep him under twenty-four-hour guard, and he was able to get away. Many cults go to greater lengths to keep their members, using sophisticated brainwashing techniques. This is why families often send in professional rescue teams to kidnap cultists and deprogram them. If you are flirting with cult life, please take a hard look at the people in it. Are they allowed to leave if they wish? Has the cult taken charge of all their money? Is dogma being promoted as enlightenment? Is a jail being offered as a protected environment? Be very suspicious of doors that don't swing both ways.

Making the Shift

Are you trying to replace fear, rage, despair, or guilt with love, joy, hope, and awe? You can do it in a more constructive way. Real passions certainly involve more than artificial experiences such as drugs, sex, and cults. If you need help in getting rid of a substance-abuse or sex habit or if a cult has a hold on you or someone you love, reach for assistance. If you do not know the name of a specific program your doctor may be able to give you a referral. Or start with your local health department. You may have to follow a trail of phone numbers to eventually arrive at your destination, but this "trip" will be worth it. (For other ideas, see Appendix.) The best programs today help you figure out what made you crave a pseudo-passion in the first place.

More Than Wishing

Even if you are not in the grip of a false passion, you still may want to know how to cultivate the real thing.

Positive passions involve more than passing coincidences.

You will hardly ever see tension or sadness on Cassandra's face. She is a skilled listener and gives great amounts of her time to working in a soup kitchen. She says she appreciates her life and is thankful every day for everything she has. She is not classically beautiful—her face is wrinkled, her hair wispy and in several colors as she transitions from light brown to gray—but many say she is beautiful nonetheless.

After you have known Cassandra for a year or so, you will find out other things about her: One of her children is profoundly schizophrenic and in an institution, and her husband left her when she was in her forties. Cassandra could have decided to protect herself from more lows by feeling no more highs—but she didn't.

How do Cassandra and other people like her remain so open to positive emotion?

Focusing They choose to focus on the good. Cheerful people are not usually complainers. Do you think they experience less pain, grief, rage, and other emotional strains than the rest of us? That is doubtful. These people tip their emotional balance in favor of joy, love, hope, awe, and other positives by keeping those uppermost in their minds and in conversation; by paying their respects to unpleasant feelings but allowing the positive ones to coexist. It can be said that emotionally successful people cultivate within themselves an artist's eye, a poet's ear, and a lover's heart.

Acceptance   Accept the bad with the good without feeling victimized. Life is a package deal: birth and death; love and hate; care and neglect. It is not possible to shut out the bad completely. Some bad things will happen to us because of random bad luck, some because of human foibles. But emotionally successful people deal with life's sad side not by wallowing in it but rather by accepting what can't be changed and *doing* something when they can: by giving time or money to causes, helping out however best they can, understanding that the job will never be done, and not taking bad luck and sad luck personally. Both can be inconvenient or even heartbreaking, but not a sign of our fate.

Self-protection   When things go wrong, do not automatically blame yourself. This would be adding insult to injury. This is not to say that emotionally successful people do not take responsibility—they certainly do. But they remind themselves that everyone makes mistakes. So do not spend days or weeks hindering your pleasure in life by going over and over past errors. And when things go right, thank yourself and give yourself some credit. Try it!

Openness   A sage once said, Seek and you shall find. The *seeking* is the more important part of this advice. Opt for openness to positive experience by saturating yourself with appropriate stimuli. Where do we look for joy, hope, awe, and other positive passions? All around us.

"I find most of my joy in the family," says Marie. "My work makes me feel competent, but watching my children learn to ride their bikes, seeing my daughter get married, coming home to find my little grandson asleep on the couch . . . these things made me feel great waves of joy.''

Marie's husband, Jack, appreciates his family too, but what brings him the most joy are accomplishments. "I remember when I passed the highest level radio operator exam," he says. "I got about half a mile down the road and then yelled, 'Yahoo!' " When the astronauts walked on the moon, when the U.S. hockey team won an Olympic medal—these are his moments of joy.

So it is in the seeking, in the doing, in the way you perceive what you do, and in the willingness to feel, that peak emotional experiences emerge. If it is joy you are pursuing, do things that you suspect might make you feel joyful. Most "love opportunities" involve interacting with people. If you know that people bring you happiness, arrange your life so that you frequently encounter people. If nature nurtures your awe, immerse yourself in it. If religion brings you hope or being with your family makes you feel love, attend religious services or be with your family. If they live far away, make them feel welcome and maybe they will come to you. Do not just think about positive emotions—create them!

Patience Once you have set the stage for your positive emotions to germinate, grow, and mature, have patience. Love, joy, and happiness do not happen in a day. It can take weeks or months. If you try to force the emotion, your experience will not be valid. This will not harm your effort, but it may disappoint you temporarily. The key to incubation is patience. Wait. Do not try to speed the process with artificial substances.

Very often after a long waiting period, you may even have forgotten what you were waiting for. Then suddenly it happens. You make a quick shift to the passion you have been hoping for. When you do, give yourself the pleasure of enjoying and reviewing your emotional experience. Check your gut reaction, your mind and body. Was it the real thing? Did it ring true? Live it and realize it.

Now Give It Away

Once you have found how to increase your own emotional opportunities, you are ready to share. When you feel something good coming on, say so. Describe it, and your audience may soon be sharing the feeling with you. You took a beautiful photo of someone? Have copies made and send them out. You are in love? Maybe you do not have to describe every detail, but love is one of those feelings that is contagious; your happiness can remind other people that life can be good. It is always wonderful at weddings to hear the vows people make to each other, and it is a time to renew them yourself if you are married. You believe there has never been a better time to be alive? Try to explain yourself. You may convince someone else.

It would be wonderful if we focused on the positive emotions instead of the negative ones we are drawn into so easily. It will be a big change. Can you imagine talking at a dinner party *not* about your fears for the economy but *instead* about the possible good that might come from new tax laws? Can you imagine discussing over coffee with friends *not* the horrible side of your mother-in-law who inserts herself into your every action but *instead* the better side of your mother-in-law who has been so supportive? If it feels strange to be so sunny, know that you will eventually become accustomed to it.

Meanwhile, you may want to encourage someone else who is negative to find the bright side of things.

Go ahead. Put me out of business—I would be positively delighted!

JOY:
Ecstasy
Without Agony

Why do so many of us have so much less joy in our life than we want? Our capacity for joy is inborn. Our experience of joy is unforgettable. Our quest for joy is endless, and our response to it is uplifting. Joy is as much a peak mind/body emotion as love or rage. According to the Passions Survey, it is one of the emotions we experience frequently, and we would like to experience more.

Is it the nature of joy that it is hard to achieve? Must we rely on lucky coincidence or divine providence beyond our control to feel it? And when it passes, must we feel so wrenched that we are almost sorry it ever came? Happily, the answers are no, no, and no!

Joy is elusive only when we make our "joy opportunities" scarce or leave them in the hands of others. Feeling that joy is out of our control, striking only a lucky few out of the blue, is a mistake—but that belief can become a self-fulfilling prophecy. The fear that joy will vanish brutally may make us destroy any joy that comes our way before we can savor it. The real truth is that we can actually increase the frequency and intensity of joy in our life.

Understanding the nature and nurture of joy is the first step. The better we understand what happens in our mind during joy, the more effectively we can set up joy opportunities. The better we understand what happens in our body during these peak moments, the more we can accept the passing of the peak as a natural transition rather than a cruel withdrawal. Let us start by measuring your own knowledge of joy.

THE JOY INFORMATION INVENTORY

True or false?

1. Babies must learn to smile.
2. Everyone's capacity for joy is basically the same.
3. The joy response probably has survival value.
4. An unhappy adolescent is likely to have less joy as an adult than a happy adolescent.
5. Joy can be an enduring state rather than a passing peak emotion.
6. The joy of sex is usually among the top three things women consider important to their happiness.
7. Being in love is more often a source of joy for women than for men.
8. Married working women often have more joy than housewives or singles.
9. Facial and behavioral signs of joy are always the same.

[Answers: (1) F, (2) F, (3) T, (4) F, (5) F, (6) F, (7) F, (8) T, (9) F.]

Are you surprised? Let us see why.

You may have made the common mistake of confusing joy with happiness. Happiness is an ongoing psychological state; joy is a passing, peak emotional experience. Happiness and joy are both positive feelings, but they do not necessarily coexist. We can be basically, steadily happy without punctuations of ecstatic joy. We can be swept up in moments of joy without feeling happy with ourselves or with life in general.

You may also not have realized that the capacity for joy develops early. Its predecessor, the capacity for pleasure, appears almost immediately. Within a few hours after birth, reports Frederick Leboyer, M.D., in his book *Birth Without Violence*, we spontaneously coo and kick in response to soothing sounds. A one-month-old baby's muscle tone will change when she hears her parents' voices; she will positively thrash with pleasure when her hands are clapped or she is nuzzled. By three months her smiles are directed toward familiar faces as they come into view.

It is during the fourth month that the turning point for joy is reached. That is when we begin to laugh out loud. Our face muscles create the universal expression of laughter, our heart and respiration rates increase, our body becomes warmer, and we utter delightful singsong sounds. As we get a little older, our body response becomes even stronger. We tremble with excitement at an unexpected delight. You do not remember your own infancy? Just picture your young sister, brother, son, or daughter stroking a puppy for the first time or receiving a surprise tickle from Grandpa's mustache. Fists flail, toddlers totter, and ecstatic squeals ring out.

As you pictured a child's joy, did you feel an inner smile beginning to form? It was a natural response. When infants smile, adults automatically smile back. This makes the baby smile more, kicking off a wonderful cycle, which ends with both participants sharing the joy of laughter and love. This back-and-forth response has enormous survival value for the human race, bonding an adult to a defenseless, vulnerable child, warding off harsh anger and punishment, and providing a shared experience both want to repeat.

These joyful exchanges activate two parts of the brain—the hypothalamus, which helps control appetite, sleep cycles, reproduction, and the limbic system, that powerful instigator of emotional responses. These parts of the brain are sometimes referred to as pleasure centers, and activating them produces mind/body sensations powerful enough to override the need for sleep, food, or even sex. In a famous experiment in the fifties, James Olds, Ph.D., and Peter Milner, Ph.D., implanted electrodes in lab animals' pleasure centers and then watched in amazement as the animals delivered self-stimulating impulses to the centers until they dropped from lack of food and sleep. Similarly, people caught up in the ecstasy of creating a painting or a poem, dancing in a religious ceremony, or competing in a sports event may drive themselves to exhaustion without realizing it.

Joy is a peak emotion, and its physiological component is of primary importance. In fact, we often identify joy largely by its physical aspects. Psychologists Stanley Schachter, Ph.D., and Jerome Singer, Ph.D., of Columbia University in New York City, demonstrated this by injecting volunteers with an adrenalinelike substance that increased heart rate, respiration, blood-vessel dilation, and muscle tone, after which subjects were put into contact with one of two groups of actors; one group had been instructed to act very happy and the other to act angry. As the injections took effect, the subjects picked up the external cues from the actors and the internal cues from their own bodies. Those who were exposed to the actors expressing positive emotions said they felt joy. If you increased the body reactions with more injections, they would probably report they felt ecstasy; if you decreased it to a state of mild arousal, they would probably think they felt happy.

Is the experience of joy the same for all of us? Probably not, says Michael Liebowitz, M.D., of the New York State Psychiatric Institute in Manhattan. Dr. Liebowitz suggests that individuals differ in their capacity to feel peak emotions, reflecting differences in their limbic pleasure centers. These differences may include the way a person's pleasure center is "wired," how easily the nerve cells react to stimulation, and the number of nerve cells linked to the center.

This does not mean our capacity for joy is strictly limited by something we cannot influence. Although we may not be able to change or even assess our limbic system's joy *readiness*, we certainly can assess and increase our life's joy *opportunities*. The more we increase the opportunities for joy in our life, the greater the number of joyful experiences we are likely to have. The more often we experience joy, the better we get at it—that is called the practice effect. As setting up opportunities for joy becomes second nature and joy itself becomes a familiar and expected emotion, we begin to drop our defenses against disappointment and stop making negative self-fulfilling prophecies. Joy comes more often and we experience it more fully.

Of course, no matter how good you become at feeling joy, you will not feel it all the time. Joy is a peak emotion, not a steady state. The increased heart and respiration rates, the vascular changes, and the warmth and flushing that are part of it *must* diminish over time to permit the body to get on with digestion, sleep, hormone production, and so on. The psychological changes must diminish as well, or routine daily functioning would be impossible. Imagine doing business accounts every day or shoveling snow for hours while you were ecstatically at one with the universe or receiving flashes of ultimate truth. Only in Doris Day movies! In reality, mind and body pause for joy. Continual joy, unlike continual happiness, would wreak havoc with daily life.

But even if we cannot have continual joy, we can have many, many moments of it—provided we do not make the mistake of leaving joy to chance. Instead, recognize that there are many types of joy and start setting up opportunities as often as you can. Here are eleven to start with:

The Joy of Triumph

You do not need to be a professional athlete to leap and shout for joy. Many ordinary men and women jump for joy all alone at home after receiving a prized college acceptance or behind a closed office door after pulling off a boardroom maneuver. This physical response expresses the delight of successful competition, the thrill of triumph. Go ahead—enjoy the freedom to win.

Jessica, a woman in her twenties, told me in a letter that she did just that:

> The law firm where I practice is so "old-boy" that when I became engaged, one of the older men asked me if that meant I'd be leaving. Can you *believe* that? The younger male lawyers, most of whom I consider my friends, call me "bitch litigator from hell." I take that as a compliment!
>
> So imagine how I felt when I recently was made a partner, a promotion I have wanted for a long time. After shaking hands decorously with the other partners, I returned to my office, closed the door, and pummeled the papers on my desk while I laughed—my way, I guess, of releasing all the tension that had built up over the years. Then I ordered a case of champagne. At the end of the day, I began opening bottles and poured champagne for everyone who wanted to share it with me.

The Joy of Mastery

Humankind's desire to master the difficult and frightening has many sources: natural curiosity, discomfort with the unpredictable, desire for the reassurance that comes with knowledge and control are a few. The little girl who has finally tied her shoes, the big girl who has commanded her computer correctly, the young man who has passed his driving test, the housewife who has earned her first paycheck, the injured athlete who has learned to negotiate the stairs on crutches, the frightened man who has gotten through two days without tranquilizers, the mature woman who has just earned a college degree—each feels the quiet, proud inner joy that strengthens self-esteem and makes it easier to meet and master the next challenge. Ed, a college student, tells how he mastered an academic subject:

Economics has never been a strong area for me, and so I decided I would force myself to take a course. In my school they offer a "pass-fail" option, so I took it. It's a great idea—it encouraged me to try something new.

How can I describe the way I felt in the class? I was lost, I was uncomfortable, I hated it. Finally, it began to be boring because I went into class *expecting* not to know what was going on. I did want to pass, though, so I subscribed to *The Wall Street Journal*, and I clipped and filed articles for weeks. I went over my notes again and again. I even had some sessions with the teaching assistant.

By the time we had the take-home, research-all-you-want final exam, I had great materials. After sweating over each question and reading and rereading my *Journal* articles, I would suddenly get a flash of understanding. I got a high grade on the final, and the teacher told me later that it was too bad I had taken the course pass-fail. It didn't matter to me. I knew what that "pass" on my transcript meant: VE day, victory in economics.

The Joy of Surprise

Terry found the living room filled with friends shouting "Happy birthday!" Ben opened his front door and found his daughter—who lives in England—wishing him Merry Christmas. In the middle of a movie, Gloria heard her longtime boyfriend say "I love you" for the first time. They felt their hearts beat more quickly, each caught their breath—but not one moved. Unlike the joy of triumph, the joy of surprise often leaves us motionless lest we scare the wonder away. We check the unexpected against reality before we even dare blink—and when we do, we may blink back tears.

The polls had just closed, but the results still were not in. Wendy and Jay had waged a passionate but clean campaign—no mudslinging. Would the voters respond to their issues-only approach?

Wendy and Jay tried not to look too worried as their supporters swirled around them at the election-night party, but they were not breathing well.

The doorbell! It was a runner just in from town hall with results in hand. He handed an envelope to Wendy and Jay, they opened it together, they looked at the numbers . . . For a moment, it was so quiet you could have heard a campaign button drop. Everyone was frozen. Wendy and Jay read and reread the numbers to themselves, then to each other. Then they smiled broadly. It was an incredible landslide in their favor. Applause broke out in every corner of the room, a cheer went up, and time moved on again.

The Joy of Safety

Think of the joy of safety as psychological social security. This joy usually comes to us when we are surrounded by family or friends. We sing Christmas carols or light Hanukkah candles in a circle of warmth; we sit among our loved ones after dinner feeling pleasantly full, accepted, protected, and esteemed. A feeling of goodness and comfort and blessing fills us, and we recognize the joy of safety. We think of how vulnerable we all are to time, distance, and illness, and our joy in this moment of safety is further heightened. We would like this childlike feeling to last forever, and when it is gone we look back on it with special tenderness.

Susie remembers a special place in the thick woods where she had retreated as a teenager. A small tree had become covered with vines, and as the tree's branches bent down, they formed a pretty bower. Susie invited her mother to her hideaway, but she never showed her brother her secret place. He and his rough-and-tumble friends would have taken it over. In the afternoon after school, Susie would carry her books out to her shelter and read for hours. Now Susie is thirty-four and called Susan. When she is worried, she closes her eyes and pretends she is safe in her little house in the underbrush.

The Joy of Reprieve

The sign of the joy of reprieve is a sigh, a deep, heartfelt sigh of relief and release. When a mammography report is negative, when a love returns, when a child is born healthy, we sigh. There seems to be a universal tendency to look up to the heavens as we do so, as if this joy could not be of entirely earthly origin. In fact, sometimes we try to make bargains with God in order to win this reprieve. Lorie felt just this way as she headed toward her doctor's office:

> Dear God, let it be benign, Lorie thought. Today she had had a biopsy that would tell her whether or not the breast lump she had found just a few days ago was cancerous or not. The biopsy was nothing compared with the monumental specter of breast cancer. She barely slept that night and awoke bleary-eyed and frightened. Getting out of bed that day was an act of heroism.
>
> When the nurse called and told her the results had been negative—no cancer—Lorie was so relieved she cried tears of relief. Then she went to bed, cuddled her pillow, and took a long, restful nap.

The Joy of Another's Joy

Like rage, despair, and infatuation, joy can come as a response to external cues as well as internal ones. Someone else's joy is a powerful cue. The greater our identification with that person or that person's experience, the greater the vicarious elation. A child's performance in a school play, a friend's marriage or promotion, a spouse's graduation—these can all be peak moments for us. Do not miss these joy opportunities by narrowing your world to yourself alone.

> Nana and Grampa knew that their four-year-old grandson, Timmy, wanted an electric train, so they set about finding the best one they could. On Christmas morning, he opened the packages

and squealed in delight: "A twain! Some twack! *More* twack!" His excitement was worth the money they had spent on this extravagant gift, because his excitement gave them a chance to relive a child's Christmas morning. They had their own joy and the joy of a child's surprise.

Adults often share a younger person's joy of mastery. Eileen describes her reaction to a scene she saw out her kitchen window:

I was washing the dishes one day, looking out the window occasionally as I do, when I saw the little five-and-a-half-year-old girl from next door coming along the road pedaling a two-wheeled bicycle with training wheels and a big red bow on the handlebars—a birthday present, I guess. Her mother trotted alongside. What touched my heart most was how hard this tiny child was struggling with her new bike, how much she wanted to command it, and how quickly she did. Soon she looked perfectly natural on the bike, and her mother was having a tough time keeping up with her. I felt a glow, a rush, a thrill—I felt a thankfulness that I had the opportunity to witness these moments of joy.

The Joy of Positive Anticipation

You awaken energized. Your heart is beating rapidly and you are not the least bit hungry. Your body tells you that you are experiencing the joy of anticipation. Sometimes this joy heralds the culmination of years of hard work, sometimes the approach of a long-awaited opportunity. We sometimes experience great anxiety along with positive anticipation as we plan a wedding or face the first day on an important job. The joy is real even when mixed with anxiety: It is the joy of great expectations.

All his life, Paul had wanted to be recognized for his skill as a chef, and now his recipe for zuppa di pesce had made him one of the few semifinalists of a national cuisine contest. The morning he was to cook in front of a panel of judges, he alternated between excitement and nervousness. When it was finally time for him to take the stage he thought he was going to faint.

But he wanted that ribbon to show his competence and his creativity. If he won, he thought, he'd have offers from restaurants throughout the country. He channeled his excitement and nervousness into preparing the dish for the judges, and he took home a blue ribbon. Every time he looks at it, the aura of excited anticipation is his again.

The Joy of Extraordinary Experience

She was orbiting the earth, watching it turn. There were no national boundaries visible, just land, sea, and sky. How would astronaut Sally Ride's view of earth have looked through your eyes? Would you have felt the joy of wonder? Extraordinary experiences lead to extraordinary joy.

The living room window of Walter's apartment had looked out onto a wall—the Berlin Wall—for many years. This wall separated Walter not only from the West German side of his beloved Berlin but also from his sister, Anna, who had successfully escaped East Germany twenty years ago.

Then the wall came down. As Walter walked briskly toward the meeting place he and Anna had agreed upon by letter, he felt alternately ecstatic and fearful: What if Anna wasn't there? What if they were awkward with each other? What if they didn't recognize each other? Then Walter spotted Anna. So familiar after all these years! A sister is always a sister. The feeling was so strong they were both astonished and enlightened. They ran toward each other and collided in a hug, crying and laughing in pure joy.

Almost anything that provides us with unexpected views of life can be a joy opportunity. Travel can be, too—not only a trip into outer space but a trip into inner space as well! We all must make room in our lives for emotional adventure; maintaining a rigid stability blocks out the possibility of joy.

The Joy of Laughter

Blind babies smile and deaf babies giggle. Laughter is not learned; it is within us. It releases pain-killing brain chemicals called endorphins and encourages the release of natural cortisone. It buffers our fears and hides our hurts. It blocks cynicism, doubt, distrust, and guilt. It often allows us to begin the climb toward joy.

Lee and her mother had had an argument and had not spoken to each other for a month. Lee found it regrettable that she desperately needed a dress she had stored in the attic of her mother's house. When she called to ask if she could come over to get the dress, her mother was barely civil.

Lee hoped her mother would let her go up to the attic alone to get the dress, but no such luck. Does she think I'm going to steal something? Lee wondered. Worse, after ten minutes of digging through piles of old clothes, she could not find the dress she wanted.

What she did find was an old tuxedo. It looked too small for anyone in the family—whose could it have been? Lee's mother had come over to look. "That was your father's," she told Lee. "The last time he wore it must have been forty years ago." She laughed at the pleasure of the memory. Lee laughed too, at the thought of her 250-pound dad ever wearing a garment this size. In one moment of shared amusement, their quarrel was forgotten and the joy of being a family was remembered.

The Joy of Faith

Science has explained many things, but for those who have religious beliefs, faith can be a constant source of healthful and helpful feelings. Listen to how spirituality has brought joy into a life where it was least expected.

It was nearly a month since the funeral, and Genie still felt overwhelming grief at the loss of her husband, Robert, a policeman who had been killed by a drug dealer. Now a home pregnancy test had confirmed her suspicions. Genie was going to have a baby. She spent the entire day crying. Never had she felt so lonely. Finally, late in the afternoon, she put on makeup and went out for a walk. As she slowly made her way down the street, she saw a loaded garbage Dumpster. Right on top of the pile of refuse, perfectly clean, was a book—the Old Testament. Genie slowly picked up the book. In it were messages about love, forgiveness, and life. Standing there on the street, Genie read the words and cried tears of joy as her thoughts turned from Robert's death to her new child's life. She felt blessed.

Genie found great solace in her Bible and its message: Focus on life and love, on what you gain, not what you lose. When the little girl she had conceived with Robert was born, she named her Roberta.

The Joy of Love

Scientists agree with songwriters: Life is better with love. In fact, in a survey Jonathan Friedman did for his book *Happy People*, single men, single women, married men, and married women all ranked love among the three factors most vital to their overall happiness. Is this mainly because love leads to sex? Apparently not. Married women ranked sex only fourth most important to happiness; single men ranked sex fifth; and both single women and married men ranked it sixth. Why does love lead to happiness? Probably because people involved in a loving relationship have more joy opportunities. The joy of love deserves its own chapter in this book. It is the next chapter. Read on.

More Joy

If your life is joyless now, you can create joy in several ways.

Rediscover the child in you Even if your childhood was grim, I believe that there is a child alive inside of you who knows how to see the world as wondrous. Learn to be joyful by finding the child in you. This does not mean you should become childish. Go back to the early times. Try to remember the joys of your youth: the first time you tasted chocolate or ice cream, the day you laughed at the funny face the dog made, the time you read poetry and "got it," the first kiss you actually liked. Look at the world today through first-time eyes. Pretend it is the first night with your lover again, that it is the first time you have been in your house, or the first day on your job. Go back to the early mornings when you were the only one up and about. What did you do? Put together a jigsaw puzzle? Did you curl up on the sofa and read? Go outside and breathe in the fresh morning air? Do it again. One way to go forward is to go back.

Borrow joy from other people Did you know we can learn to be joyful? One way is through *modeling*, through imitating behavior we see working for others. To learn joy through modeling, place yourself in the company of people who know how to be joyful. Choose a friend with the lightest laugh, the biggest smile, the warmest hug. Spend extra time with her alone. Watch how she responds to little disasters. Chances are she knows how to find the humor in any situation. Are the two of you the same or different? Tell her about your latest little disaster and see if she spots joy that you missed. Next week, after your next unjoyful event, have the dialog with yourself. See it through her eyes. Soon her joyful point of view will become yours.

Now, start your own joy diary   Once you are feeling small bursts of joy, you are ready to make more. Start a diary, which will be a record of the joys you feel. This will be a special book only for those special feelings. They do not need to be big joys: the quick smile you felt when you saw soldiers returning from the war deserves to be in your book of joy too, and the triumph you felt when you finally learned to master the Stairmaster in your exercise gym. If you keep a diary, several things will happen:

• You will recognize the joys that are already in your life. Soon joyful moments will not slip by unnoticed.
• You will reinforce your joy behavior. Each time you catch yourself feeling joy, you will feel you have won another prize.

You will learn which of the eleven joys we have covered in this chapter feel best to you. You may even discover a few new joys! Then you can cultivate more joy by arranging your life so that more joy will be likely. If your greatest source of joy is always that of other people, you know for sure that by directing some of your leisure time into helping the aged, the homeless, infertile women, or abused children, you will almost certainly guarantee your own personal brand of joy. If your joy comes from moments of solitude, find the time to create more islands of that kind of joy.

If you look at your book of joy and see that there are periods where you have made no entries, ask yourself what happened. Were there no joy opportunities? Were you too distracted? Was there too much pain in your life? Did you feel unentitled to joy because somebody in your life was feeling pain? Some women tell me that when they are overweight, they do not permit themselves any joy. Other people torture themselves when they have fallen behind at work and do not stop torturing themselves until they are caught up.

For joy to be a permanent part of your life, it cannot depend upon outside circumstances. Make joy a permanent part of *you*! Wake up every morning knowing that there already is joy potential inside you and all you need to find are opportunities to feel it. And then the joys that come by surprise will be the "extras," not the "onlies."

LOVE: Song of the Soul

We love love. We love to give it; we love to get it. It makes us feel generous, strong, and devoted. Life suddenly has meaning! Love connects us to another person body to body, mind to mind, soul to soul. Love is the only emotion that has its own holiday—Valentine's Day.

Love has so many splendors that the ancients describe at least ten variations on the theme. If some names of these types of love are Greek to you, that is because they are indeed Greek words, thousands of years old.

storge—devoted love	*narcissus*—self centered love
caritas—respectful love	*agape*—spiritual love
pragma—convenient love	*philia*—friendly love
ludus—flirtatious love	*mania*—maddened love
eros—fascinated love	*lust*—sexual love

As unique as our personal love stories may seem to us, history tells us that for centuries, people have been captured by this peak mind/body emotion—leaving their songs, stories, poems, and love letters behind to dignify and immortalize their passion.

Love may be old, but for each of us it is brand new. Even if we have loved before, we can have an experience that amazes us. The most experienced lover can find herself swept away on new tides of emotion. The most jaded womanizer can be awakened by a sudden, unfamiliar feeling of . . . could it be love this time? *Real* love? Maybe love is always new because there are so many different kinds. If you have felt one or two, you have not felt them all.

All types of love are passions, but some are more intense than others. During intense loves, the mind feels obsessed and the body feels possessed. But during "gentle loves" the feelings create more of a presence than an altered state of consciousness. Let's see what they are like.

The Gentle Loves

Some loves are mainly of the mind, flavored by affection, appreciation, or amusement, and unaccompanied by body changes, confusion, or earth-shattering obsession. We can ponder, wonder, and muse. Our pupils will not dilate and our palms will not sweat. Subtle brain-wave patterns may suggest that we are contemplating love rather than sleeping or leaping, but our digestion patterns will not be changed. The gentle loves are: devoted, respectful, friendly, self-centered, spiritual, and flirtatious.

Devoted love is lasting love, and because it lasts, it cannot maintain itself at a constant peak. It differs from intense passion in many specific ways. Intense passions like infatuation interfere with our concentration at school, work, or home; devoted love helps us toward higher achievement. Infatuation can be based on external characteristics; love that lasts is based on inner character. Infatuation can occur when opposites attract, but devoted attraction is based on similarities.

The function and nature of devoted love, then, is very different from the function and nature of infatuation. Intense passion is likely to help us escape from daily life for a while. Devotion helps us manage daily life and share our view of reality. Intense passion gets us into a relationship. Devotions helps us stay in a relationship.

One good place to look for models of devoted love is in actual couples you know. Do the stable real-life couples you admire most live in a haze of romance? Maybe they did in the first six months of their affair, but love that endures and relationships that last have more to do with shared values than with flowers or candy.

Sharing points of view turns out to be the best predictor of long-term bonding. What were stimulating debates on dates turn into tedious arguments at home if the issues are family, money, or marriage. The extras may count in intense passion, but it is the basics that count in devoted love. The color of a man's eyes, the wave of his hair, and the cut of his suit cannot predict his capacity for commitment or his sense of responsibility. Watch his behavior instead. Observe his friendships and family relationships. Make sure your compatibility extends beyond the dance floor and bedroom. Love is not blind—intense passion is!

Love for a child is another kind of love that endures, a special kind of devoted attraction. People who thought they knew all about love are often surprised when they first feel love for their child. It is different, sweeter, and more giving. You find the child beautiful, and his or her vulnerability makes you feel protective. When the child is not with you, perhaps you yearn to see his little fingers or hear about her day. From the moment they are born, our young ones give love: At first they cling, and by one year of age they are smiling and openly affectionate. It is often irresistible. For people who have avoided feeling love, a child can open the door.

So can *respect*. Respect is a kind of love. It often appears in long marriages, old friendships, and teacher/student and mentor/apprentice relationships. Respectful love often brings together people who might otherwise never have met or become close.

We have the capacity to find another gentle love in some very unlikely places. You have perhaps heard stories of society women who fall in love with their bodyguards and tales of prisoners who come to love their captors.

When you were young, did you feel as though your best friend was the most important person in your life? Maybe even more important than your mother or father? As we grow older, *friendly love* remains important: In a world that changes all the time, an old friendship can be the rock of ages. Marriage counselors say that the best marriages are built on a foundation of friendship.

Friendships begin all kinds of ways. Sometimes two people meet as equals; sometimes one person is attracted to the other and pursues the friendship. Friendships often begin on common ground: You both like motorcycles, you both have hyperactive children, you are both passionate about hating your boss. Sometimes two people come together because of an X factor—we do not know what the similarity is, but we know we are soul mates. Friends like these sometimes spend hours trying to analyze their friendship but never get very far. Knowing why a friendship works is probably good information about ourselves but not essential to the friendship.

With friendship comes affection. Affection is love in an everyday, practical form. We show affection by a pat on the head, a smile, a simple "I like you." Like friendship, affection is for somebody you know well. Many couples who married for intensely passionate reasons discover that affection for each other grows, too—and often outlasts the initial passion!

A little *self-love* is not a bad thing either. The world is not going to take your love pulse every few days to make sure you are getting enough, and self-love may be an important antidote to that. A single woman I know buys herself chocolates, fine china, and other presents that people usually give to show love or to recognize marriage. She takes herself out to brunch once in a while and awards herself a week in a spa each year. She does not pity or blame herself for her solitary life-style. This type of self-love is healthy. We all need love, and because our single friend's need is not met another way, she is taking good care of herself. Her satisfaction makes it easier for her to give love, too.

The self-centered attraction we call narcissism, however, is a futile pursuit. Narcissus was the name of a beautiful boy who saw his reflection in a pool and fell in love with it. Every time he tried to touch this wonderful face, the image fell into fragments, and Narcissus could never have his love. There is a paradox in too much self-love. Although we are pouring love into ourselves, we can end up feeling oddly empty. We can feel full only when we give love away, as in the next type of love, which is the opposite of narcissistic love.

The ideal of loving without judging or expecting anything was called *agape* by the ancient Greeks. Can we ever love so freely and unreservedly? Though we may love our children, our parents, and our friends this way, can we extend agape to strange people, dirty people, people who take instead of give? This special love is one that most religions would say you can learn to feel if you want it enough. The requirements are a sincere desire to experience this type of love and constant practice.

But many human characteristics stand in the way of agape. People feel safer in small groups that exclude unfamiliar others. We are able to love someone specific, such as a person we know, but we have trouble with conceptual loving. Finally, we are used to bestowing love as a reward. We often think that certain people do not deserve this reward from us.

Though we do not all aspire to it, we all have the capacity for *some* agape. If we study the wisdom that has preceded us, if we imitate models of agape such as Mother Theresa, if we desire it enough, we can move closer to spiritual love as a goal, if not a reality.

At its best, *flirtatious love* is some of the best fun adult people can have. It is a compliment to the person we are flirting with. It is a way to tell someone that we find him or her attractive enough to know more deeply. It is also a way to ask someone if he or she considers us to have the same potential. Usually, flirting is harmless play, a simple sign of human interest, and both parties interpret it that way. Sometimes we misuse flirting. If we are insecure, we may ask for the response too often and lose interest just when interest is beginning to grow in the object of our flirtation. With the right person at the right moment, however, flirting can be a spark that lights a fire in two people at the same time, sending them on a journey into other kinds of love.

The Passionate Loves

The gentle loves are mainly of the mind—flavored largely with thoughts of affection, amusement, or appreciation. But the passionate loves are in our physical being as well as our mind. They are *infatuation, erotic love,* and *sexual love.* They energize us. They make us feel young if we are mature, and wise if we are young. They create a temporary psychoticlike state in which reality has been left behind. Adults have delusions of childlike dependency, phone calls are tainted with life and death urgency, and our lover's approval seems necessary for our very survival . . .

When poets, songwriters, and artists exalt love, it is usually *infatuation* that they are talking about. Although infatuation isn't really love, we usually love it anyway. From eighteen to eighty-nine, we become infatuated and remember our affairs always. In fact, the Passion Survey respondents said that regardless of how the affair turned out, in retrospect their infatuation was a positive experience.

How can you tell whether you are in love or in infatuation while you are in the midst of an experience? Use the guide that follows.

(Men, please substitute "her" for "him" throughout.)

LASTING LOVE—OR INFATUATION?

You see him as the essence of attractiveness and *worry* that he's irresistible to others.

It's infatuation.

You see him as attractive to you and you feel *secure* when you are with others.

It's love.

You spend a great deal of time *fantasizing* about the future.

It's infatuation.

You spend a great deal of time *planning* for the future.

It's love.

Every step feels like *destiny* and every coincidence like mystical "meant-to-be"s.

It's infatuation.

Every step feels like a *choice* and happily-ever-after is today.

It's love.

He is living proof that *opposites* attract.

It's infatuation.

He is living proof that *similarities* in values are important.

It's love.

You love him but don't like him.
Your feelings are intensified by *conflict*.

It's infatuation.

You love him and like him.
Your feelings are perpetuated by *friendship*

It's love.

You are *distracted* and unable to sleep:
You can't proceed with your daily life until he has called.

It's infatuation.

You are *focused* and sleep like a baby:
You can't wait to tell him about your achievements.

It's love.

It's a *one-sided* passion.

It's infatuation.

It's a *mutual* experience.

It's love.

The characteristics of infatuation and love are not only different, they are often diametrically opposed. Love helps us realize ourselves and share our view of reality. Infatuation helps us pretend we are different by being with someone who is different. Love is bonding, each new one is unique. Infatuation is addictive, each new one curing the last. Love combines joy and trust. Infatuation combines pleasure and *fear*. During infatuation, the brain sends signals to the body that the loss of the loved one is as life-threatening as the loss of the nurturing parent would be to a helpless infant. Your sympathetic nervous system gears up as it would for an emergency. Adrenaline pours into your bloodstream. Your muscle tone changes from relaxed to ready for fight or flight. Your heart, lungs, intestines, sweat glands, blood vessels, liver, kidneys, and endocrine glands all respond to autonomic nervous system messages, which originate in your brain. Considering the strong physical reaction we can have to the idea of love lost, it is no wonder that jealousy can make us tremble and obstacles can stimulate even more energetic pursuit.

Because it agitates both body and mind, an up-and-down infatuation eventually will wear us out. It will strip us of our reserves of blood sugar, adrenaline, and hope. So we reach for coffee, cola, and sweets to replace fantasies and phone calls. But when these quick fixes stimulate the production of too much insulin, blood sugar levels drop and physical fatigue is added to psychological depression. And then, like a drug addict longing for another fix, we look for a new infatuation to pull us out of this unhappy state.

What to Do When the Thrill Is Gone

A better idea than looking for a new infatuation is a mind-and-body vacation *from* infatuation.

- Spend some time trying to decide why you gave him so much power over your feelings and behavior. Was he parental? A benevolent dictator? Did she treat you in a way that made you feel she knew the "real" you—for better or worse? Whatever the reasons, you gave him that power; you can take it back!
- Review the way you saw yourself and him during the infatuation. Did he seem to have a characteristic you always wanted to have yourself? Did you perceive him as better than you rather than just different? If so, you were being critical of yourself. Try being descriptive, instead. Know who you *are* rather than who you think you *should* be.
- Don't confuse aggravation with infatuation. "I must really care if I feel so upset" is not an example of clear thinking.
- Reassess her behavior in terms of information about her, not as information about her feelings toward you. What did her behavior reveal about her attitudes, considerations or intelligence? Was she as "ideal" as you had probably imagined? If you had not been the man involved, what would you have thought of her behavior?
- Become your own loved one. Take good care of yourself until your perspective and energy are restored. Treat yourself just as you would have liked him to treat you. Reassure yourself that you are worth it.

Why are we talking about infatuation as if it is invariably doomed? Are there no happy endings? Is there no such thing as lasting love at first sight? Yes, there can be a happy outcome for those who fall in love at first sight if they also share values and go on to share experiences. Infatuation can *lead* to lasting love over time. Just as often, though, infatuation is a sweet cheat that deceives in a way we cannot understand until the infatuation has come to an end.

I'm crazy about him, thought Robynn. And crazy was right. She was a woman married to a good man who was busy starting up a business. Maybe the long hours alone had triggered Robynn's giant crush on Eddie, a much younger man. Eddie seemed to know that she needed attention, and he gave it: He and Robynn went to lunch, took long walks, talked for hours on the phone. She lost her appetite, dropped a few pounds, went to sleep late, woke up early, and spent hours daydreaming about Eddie.

Robynn agonized about whether or not to sleep with Eddie. Sometimes their telephone conversations were so sexy to her that Robynn felt as though they *had* made love. But Eddie did not press her for sex. In fact, Robynn thought he seemed reluctant. This made Robynn feel safe. How wise she thought Eddie was. How much he understood.

How did it end? Robynn became pregnant—by her husband. Her hours alone were now filled with baby preparations and plans. The pregnancy changed her view of the relationship with Eddie, but Eddie didn't seem to mind. Perhaps he had always seen her as a friend.

One way love can also be a peak experience, and some people pursue it for the lift and distraction from routine. In fact, it is possible to have the physical and emotional turbulence of infatuation without *any* response from another person. But this unrequited love is usually more pain than pleasure—ultimately an empty experience.

Though it may be hard advice to take, the prescription for such maddened love is interruption and evaluation. The obsessed person must create physical distance between himself or herself and the object of the obsession and then examine why he or she chose to pursue someone who is inaccessible. For some, group therapy can provide answers and a built-in support system. For others, individual therapy can help change these self-defeating behaviors.

When the excitement of infatuation blends with a physical interlocking, that is *erotic love*. Time stops, surroundings recede—the two lovers *become* time and place as they plunge into deep emotional and physical pleasure. Erotic love can be so far from our normal condition that it becomes remarkable, transcendant, and unforgettable. Eros is a passion many seek and hope to keep forever.

Two years ago, Ernest and Candace met at a dinner party. Immediately, Ernest knew what lay ahead—a long, passionate romance. As if by telepathy, before they said much, he and his new love knew they both felt the same way. For several intensely pleasurable hours they talked quietly, until the party was over.

That night as they made love, they felt their own pleasure and each other's pleasure too. They were so close that it was natural for each to know what the other wanted. Their bodies and feelings twisted and twined together like vines growing in a garden of love. Now, two years later, their love life is still extraordinarily erotic in flavor, though less driven. The discoveries they have made about themselves and each other have kept them physically and emotionally close.

Like infatuation, erotic love causes a swelling of emotions. Our mental and physical arousal combine to increase hormones that uplift us. During arousal and at its erotic peak, orgasm, our bodies become flooded with biochemicals that make us feel wonderful. Then the tide of hormones—cortisone, endorphins, adrenaline—subsides, and we carry residues of the feelings with us as we do other things. Eros is certainly one of the most memorable passions.

Infatuation and erotic love are similar but not identical. When an infatuation ends, our minds and bodies go through a withdrawal from the thoughts and love chemicals we have become accustomed to; we eventually realize that what we were experiencing was a pleasant delusion.

When an erotic love relationship ends, it is a real loss. If you not only loved someone's company but you loved the sex, the way your bodies felt together, then the missing can be excruciating, as if you lost a part of yourself. Because of this potential pain, many people try to confine themselves to lust without love.

Whether you think *lust* is to be enjoyed or to be resisted, you probably agree that it has a strong pull on almost all of us. Long ago, when mating may have meant that a caveman swept the cavewoman of his choice off her feet and carried her to a secluded spot for sex, lust assured the future of the human race. Society eventually came down hard on lust. It is not kind or practical or healthy to put every attraction into action. Nor is lust the driving force behind most long-lasting relationships. But lust can still live on as part of a good sexual and emotional relationship.

Lust may be body love, but its origin is in the *mind*. The brain fixates and the body vibrates. Sexual commentators have said that the brain is the sexiest part of the body, because in lust, as in other forms of passionate love, the brain is running the show. Once the brain has granted permission, our bodies take over. In other words, lust is for mutually consenting adults only.

> Jennifer is in her thirties and feels she has reached her sexual maturity—"Finally! After all those years of guilt and inhibition!" she says. If she has a sexy thought about her husband when they are together, Jennifer no longer blushes or tries to distract herself—she tells Rick about it. Or does something about it: She has been known to come up and caress Rick's shoulders or whatever other body part she was thinking of at the time. And when he comes up and strokes her, instead of wiggling out of his grasp or saying something evasive the way she used to, she settles into the feeling and allows his touch to turn her on. Rick and Jennifer have made love in every room of their apartment, including the balcony, and show no signs of losing interest in their hobby.

Sometimes lust plays itself out. What once seemed so healthy and robust seems to have vanished and we cannot summon it back. But the loss of lust is not a pain we feel in every fiber, like the loss of erotic love. Part of the reason is that it has not occupied every fiber, like erotic love. Lust is more a body passion than a mind one, and once we have experienced it a few times, we can understand that easily.

But lust can hurt in an indirect way. For many women, lust does not stay lust—it slowly evolves into other forms of love that are harder to give up.

Samantha had always found Tom attractive, and finally she caught his attention. She soon found out that this was a man with intense sexual drives who was capable of making her melt with just a look. They lived in the same part of the city, and often, on his way home from work, he would come to Samantha's apartment, hang around for a while, give her that look . . . the sex was the best. Often they fell asleep in her bed, arms around each other.

But in the morning his side of the bed was always empty and cool. Samantha began to wish he would stay and let her make him breakfast. She began to wonder why he never invited her to go anywhere with him. She realized that she was beginning to love him in a way he could not return just then. So she told him, "No more. You're hurting me." They talked, and he began to understand. Year later, they are friends and remember their good times fondly.

Women—and most men too—need afterplay as well as foreplay!

It is part of living lusty lives. I do not mean that they fall into bed with every delivery man who comes through the door. I mean their lust can extend beyond sex to become a lust for wonderful food, good friends, beautiful art, all of life itself. It is something we not only can look forward to with pleasure but can also plan for. Start practicing a lust for life now. Have a love affair with music, gymnastics, history, or mystery novels; become more passionate about the plight of the elderly, disabled children, perhaps the homeless. And next time you make love, do it with gusto.

What Is Not Love

Love has many splendors, and it also has many unrelated imposters. Emotions that often pose as love are:

Sexual addiction   As we said earlier in the book, someone who constantly pursues sexual experiences in order to release tension is addicted to the biochemicals of love: endorphins, norepinephrine, dopamine, serotonin, and phenylethylamine, which make us feel optimistic and energetic. This addiction is more than just lust. The addict uses sex to feel less lonely, less angry, more defiant, or more self-assured. The sex may be compulsive and unfulfilling—a trap for the person who so desperately wants to feel better instead of worse!

The double standard that still lives on leads many to think of men who fix all their tension with sex as passionate "studs" but women who operate the same way as "weak" or "easy." Among the hundreds of men and women I surveyed last year about this type of dependency, I heard men labeling their compulsive sexual behavior as "recreational." Men may even flout insatiable sexual passion as they would the capacity to hold liquor or lose big at gambling without flinching.

Women tell me another story. They see their problems with compulsive sex as something they should keep secret. They call it "humiliating." So do many men:

> Chris does not feel satisfied even after many orgasms. He is ashamed to say that he masturbates several times a day. He fears that his wife is overwhelmed by his insatiability, as he is. He feels out of control. He does not blame his wife, he insists, because the problem started before he met her and he considers her "a terrific lover."

Although the incidence of compulsive behavior in our population cannot be reliably measured, it was discussed as primarily a "female" problem in most of the research literature until the AIDS epidemic. Now that gay and bisexual men are seeking to save their lives by controlling sexual compulsions, it is becoming clearer that sexually compulsive behavior is probably not related to gender. Men and women alike are susceptible to this household remedy for feelings of inner emptiness. Since women are not expected to be masturbating during their morning shower or having "matinees" during the day, since they are not expected to need the services of prostitution, pornography, or massage parlors, and since they rarely "keep" a sexual partner in the style to which he would like to be accustomed, the woman who is sexually compulsive has double trouble: Fewer opportunities mean more anxiety, and greater shame means more self-punishment.

The medical students I have taught seem to be particularly fascinated with this pseudopassion, and they are often concerned about the criteria for diagnosis. "Does the diagnosis apply if the compulsion is situational or transient?" they ask every year. "Are you wondering about yourself?" I always ask. "A friend," they of course reply. And then I tell them what they want to know. The problem can be situational. The seductive anonymity of travel, conventions, demonstrations, or military service can trigger hypersexuality. Sexual passion can be a temporary distraction from preoccupation with someone back home. Sexual closeness with strangers in the night may reflect extreme anxiety about being wrenched from familiar surroundings. As on our first day at school, we may be fighting separation terror. Instead of reaching for a loved one, we *create* one through instant intimacy and carry our passion with us to keep us warm.

Many kinds of life changes also encourage passing sexual passion. Changing a job, moving, and starting a new school can be opportunities for new contact without old restraints. But remember, the first impressions you make can last a very long time. Many patients work long and hard in therapy in order to deal with the problems that resulted from a brief episode of compulsive sexuality and its cause. Many women tell me that they changed colleges after being sexually insatiable their freshman year. Many men tell me that they had to unwillingly change wives or careers after sexual indiscretions in a new city or on a new job.

This does not mean that every period of increased sexual activity should be suspect. But if each experience seems to be a cure for the last disaster and each feels more familiar than unique, I suggest a pause. If satisfaction is brief even when the sex is "terrific," and lulls in sexual activity create anxiety, I suggest that you ask yourself what need the sex may be serving, then search to serve your needs better. When many men and women reach mid-life, as an example, they tell me that their libido becomes uncontrollable—as does their sexual behavior. Some describe it as a "last-chance" syndrome. Others say that they want a "do-over." All are probably trying to control anxiety associated with aging. Since the hallmark of all pseudopassions is denial, the first step toward serving your needs better is complete honesty.

Let me say once again that more than willpower is usually needed to regain a sense of choice and control over any dependency. Reach for insight and behavior modification, also. A driven libido can be a sign of a failing attempt to solve a problem: fear of intimacy, fear of isolation, fear of aging, to name a few.

Other love imposters:

Need We often confuse our need for someone with love.

Tony had never felt quite so sick—this flu was a killer. Flat on his back, Tony had to depend upon Lilly, his live-in girlfriend, to bring him soup, toast, and aspirin, which she did tirelessly. She even stayed home from work to take care of him. Tony was grateful. While she rubbed his back, he said, "I love you, Lilly." It was the first time she had heard him say that. It was also the last.

Even when we are healthy, we need others, and we can feel immensely grateful to someone who fills that need. Need and love are almost opposites. In need, instead of giving love, we are asking for it. Needing someone is not a crime, but it is not love either.

Distance and pursuit We often fall in love with someone who is at a physical remove. Teenage girls adore rock stars; men worship movie actresses. Falling in love with someone from a distance can mean several things. We may be practicing for real love; we may be avoiding real love because we feel afraid, unworthy, or inexperienced; or we may be in love not with a real person but with a creation we have imbued with unreal, perfect qualities. Love at a distance is only an illusion of love.

When we are not content to admire our long-distance lover from afar and have the opportunity, we may pursue our image of perfection. The chase floods us with adrenaline, one of the hormones of passionate love. But soon as we try to match the perfect lover we have created with the real person, who is inevitably full of faults, we become disillusioned. Our illusion literally falls to pieces, and so may we. The chase and an ultimate victory ("winning" the one we think we love) are both exciting, but they are not love.

More Love in Your Life

If you would like more love in your life, here is how to enhance the nonpassionate love that already exists, recognize passion potential, and even create passionate love.

Accept love Somebody may be trying to love you at this very moment. Who could it be? Maybe someone who lives in your neighborhood, someone at work, or someone in a group you belong to. This person may be offering you a nonpassionate love based on shared interests, understanding, admiration, or other quiet virtues. Allow yourself the luxury of accepting this kind, patient human love. It can blossom.

Give love Many of us feel we do not have much love to give. Other people look forbidding to us. We wonder why we should bother. We wonder if they will interpret our intention the wrong way. We feel superior or inferior to these other creatures who intrude on our space.

To cultivate love, start from the other side. What is it about each person that you could love, however insignificant? Perhaps a sense of humor or a small talent you see. This can be the beginning of a greater experience for you to enjoy.

Express love   Send valentines in August. Call up and chat for no reason. Make an effort to put yourself in someone else's place and let him or her know you understand. Touch. Hug. Kiss. Give someone a nickname. Say ''I love you'' to someone you love.

Imagine love lost   It is a funny thing about family—we know we are supposed to love our husbands, wives, and significant others, and yet we often do not really feel it until something stands in its way. This wife never loved her husband as much as when she thought she was losing him.

> One day at work, Jack had the feeling time had stopped. He searched for his pulse and decided it was his heart that had stopped instead. He stood up, walked down the hall to the infirmary, and told the nurse. Then he lay down on the nearest cot and passed out. As the nurse searched his chest with a stethoscope for some sign of life, Jack's blood pressure returned to normal, and soon he came out of his faint.
>
> On her way to the plant to pick Jack up, his wife Marie felt many strong emotions. Marie imagined life without him. How many times, when he had been critical of her, she had wished he would just dry up and blow away. Now that she might really be about to lose him, she remembered those warm, wonderful days of sailing on the bay before they had been married. She saw him with their oldest little girl on his lap as he showed her how to use a compass. She reconstructed in her mind, room by room, the house he had built for them all. The love she felt swelling up inside was almost painful, as if it were too big for her own heart, trying to get out.

If you doubt your love for people who are supposed to be "loved ones," put yourself in Marie's place. We are stubborn creatures who do not like to hear that we may not have our love, but sometimes a chance to think about someone else from a psychological distance can awaken strong physical and emotional love.

Imagine losing your opportunity to love   Sometimes it may take a cataclysmic event to open our eyes to what a gift our own lives are to others.

> After his heart attack and bypass operation, Zach found that his attitude about people had changed. "I'm so grateful to be alive," he says. "I'm much more loving toward my wife, more interested in *life*. I feel like a lot of my hangups have disappeared. I don't care what other people think anymore when I kiss my wife in the middle of a crowded party. *They're* the ones who don't know what's important."

I am not recommending that all of us engineer a life-threatening event to shake us up and realign our emotions! But if we can just imagine for a moment not being here, not having the chance to show someone our love . . . what would we tell someone if we were about to leave them forever? What would we show them? Right now you have a precious chance to release a flood of love.

Be willing to be vulnerable   Sometimes we cannot feel love because we cannot allow ourselves to be vulnerable. When we allow ourselves to love and be loved, we risk losing that love. That means intolerable pain to some of us, pain that we will go to great lengths to avoid. It helps to remember that just as passionate love does not last forever, the agony of loss also ends in time.

Sometimes we avoid feeling love because we fear that vulnerability can hurt us. We fear that loving means sharing, and sharing means feeling someone else's strife and pain. We fear that loving means caring and that may mean letting go. These are legitimate fears; people in the "helping professions" (nurses, social workers, ministers, priests, psychiatrists, and psychologists among them) may burn out if they try to satisfy everyone's needs. Giving love of any kind—from simple friendship to the most passionate love—means that you indeed make yourself vulnerable.

If you cannot stand the pain of vulnerability, the decision to step back for a moment is one you can make at any time: make it because you are taking care of yourself the way a mother or father would take care of you. This is called self-parenting. Are we all good self-parents all of the time? Of course not. Sometimes we let ourselves get hurt in love because we crave the luxury of love and do not think about consequences. We go into love affairs with one hand over our eyes, telling ourselves that the love is bigger than we are. We invoke these and a million other clichés so we can take our love and run away with it. Other times we let ourselves get hurt because we feel another's hurt. This is the time when we most need to listen closely to friends and other parent stand-ins who care about us. Although vulnerability may be part of love, it is not the whole of love.

Finally . . .

Love for the joy of loving   Love does not need a reason to exist. It is a capacity that does not need justification or even thought. My cat, Crystal, and my daughter, Kimberly, know about unconditional love. When he hears her keys in the lock, he bounds to the door and waits. When she comes in, she always stops to pet him and give him a nose-to-nose kiss. He likes to be touched, so she strokes him whenever she has a free hand. Whenever she eats, she feeds him too. Her love is a gift that she gives over and over again. Crystal does not have to earn it. That is why I call it a gift.

You may be reluctant to give unconditional love because you may not get it back. So what if you do not? What did it cost you? Very little, since emotions are free and there is more love in your heart. As soon as you give this delightful present away, another one will grow in your heart, wrapped and ready so you can give again. If it is not appreciated, find those who will love your love. Do not deprive yourself of the joy of loving. The capacity is yours.

HOPE:
Mind's Magic

Hope is the most magical of passions. We start with nothing, and then with the wave of a wand, something appears—a dream better than reality.

Have you ever played peek-a-boo with a one-year-old? You hide your face behind a pillow and the child pulls the pillow away in hope of finding your face again. He does, and shrieks with delight at it. Hope is fulfilled. He will now dare to hope again.

Babies are born with the *capacity* to hope, but hope cannot develop until the capacity for imagery has developed. Imagery is the ability to imagine or remember. An infant cannot hope for Mother's return if he cannot yet retain an image of Mother. As imagery develops in the first year, so does the ability to play the peek-a-boo game. Before imagery, our baby looks confused or sad or indifferent when we hide our face behind a pillow because when Mother leaves from view, Mother no longer exists for a newborn. With imagery, the baby remembers our face, pictures it behind the pillow, and reaches for the pillow. She now hopes we are still there and pulls the pillow away to make her hope come true. The ability to imagine has allowed the capacity for hope to emerge.

The feeling that we can make things happen if only we can find the right incantation, the right ceremony, or the magic words is an essense of hope. A boy sneezes, and when he opens his eyes he sees his birthday present, for a long time afterward, he may hope for a present whenever he sneezes. A girl got her first A on a spelling test the day she used a red pen; she might have just gained a lucky pen. We adults foster feelings of hope in our children. A little girl who hopes for a doll and makes her desire known may get what she wants: It might give her parents or grandparents pleasure to please her, and we like to preserve in our young the belief that dreams can come true. We are born with the capacity for hope; we learn to use it so early that it becomes part of most of us for the rest of our lives. If you feel you have lost your capacity, here is how you can begin to rediscover hope.

Passionate Hope

Hope is more than mere wanting. When you want, you feel a lack in your life and would like it filled. Wanting is in the mind. When you hope, you add to your feeling of emptiness a *vision* of the thing you want; the thing you want becomes so real you try to approach it physically.

Consider the lottery. People do not merely *want* to win $30 million. We are not just *eager* to win it or *optimistic* about it. We yearn, we burn, we cry; we hope. We clench our fists, shut our eyes tightly, breathe more quickly, and perhaps even perspire as we imagine the beach house, the Maserati, the feeling of security, the gifts we would give, and the investment portfolio that will one day be ours. We buy one lottery ticket, and if the waiting is too painful, we take more action to move toward our vision: We buy another and another, until we hit a limit of funds or conscience.

Hope is often intensified by the threat of despair, its emotional opposite. Who buys the most lottery tickets? Probably people with fewer resources of their own. We yearn for love when we are loveless, health in times of illness, peace in times of war.

As a laboratory scientist, Max is accustomed to seeing his hopes become real. New research comes out of his high-powered lab weekly, most of the findings ones that society can use for better communications or health.

Max is painfully aware that his work also applies beyond earthly limits. He sees our earth as a living planet, possibly the only one that exists anywhere. "We are the hope of the universe," he says. Each time his company's management cuts back on the basic research that Max believes could lead us to know our place in that universe, he is about to sink into despair—and then his hope returns renewed, fueling his fight for funding.

A Self-Fulfilling Prophecy

When we are hopeless, we convince not only ourselves but everyone around us that hope is not worth wasting energy on, and our inertia makes it true. When we are hopeful, we approach life and its problems with strategical behavior and our results justify our hope:

Kevin and Sarah needed money badly: They had just bought a house and were seriously overextended. Sarah suggested they sell the older of their two cars. "Nobody would ever buy that piece of junk," said Kevin. The eight-year-old Fiat sat in the driveway for a month, and sure enough, nobody bought it.

One morning when Kevin was at work, Sarah posted a sign on the car: FOR SALE; BEST OFFER. By nightfall she had a promise of $500 from a neighbor who had been eyeing the car but had not known it was for sale.

Hope led Sarah to *do something* that turned her wish into cash. Because hope is a passion—it has a physical component, action—it brings us closer to our goals.

Hope and Health

The self-fulfilling nature of hope can be especially important when we are ill. I am not calling hope a medicine—not exactly. But your hope can prime a subtle interplay of emotions between you and other people that can ultimately help to heal you. Hope can make you the kind of person that people want to help. In the case of Meyer, an eighty-seven-year-old with severe arthritis, hope attracted attention that was therapeutic.

Meyer was a favorite with the nurses at the rehabilitation center. This man, in such pain and trouble, seemed to think of the future with a smile. When his exercises hurt him and the nurses apologized, he made them feel better. His hopeful attitude about the future gave them all courage: If this fragile old man was so determined to get better, life must be worth living.

As a result of his cheerful, inspiring attitude, Meyer frequently found himself the recipient of little gifts and special considerations. The nurses frequently stopped by his room to visit, and they were more than willing to fill his needs, because it seemed so worthwhile. By keeping his spirits high, Meyer attracted the best care possible.

Hope can also lead to medical action that can change our future.

Ovarian cancer: It is one of the worst diagnoses that a woman can hear. Beth could not believe she was hearing it now. She had never thought much about her future, but suddenly it seemed that all she had ever wanted was to have a normal life, to have a family, to live. All that was at risk now.

She raged. She feared. She cried. Finally, she settled into a quiet hope, a strong almost-certainty that she would somehow get over the cancer. Her hope led her to look for the most aggressive treatments she could find, and she submitted to them almost cheerfully.

Today Beth has passed the five-year mark and is out of danger. She is married, has a baby boy, and is currently traveling with her family in Europe, something she has always wanted to do.

Hope may even have more direct health benefits. Sometimes hope about our health is well founded and sometimes it is not, but you may be amazed to know that either way, it appears to have value. Here is hope at its most passionate, an emotion clearly commanding both mind and body.

Phyllis had not been feeling well for months. She was having terrible trouble getting up to go to work, and her supervisor was beginning to talk of docking her pay for lateness. At night, she had only enough energy to eat a yogurt and collapse into bed. The doctors suspected that she was in the early stages of multiple sclerosis, but tests had not proven anything.

Then Phyllis heard about a fish diet that had worked for some people whose symptoms resembled hers. Excitedly, she began taking fish-oil capsules in the morning and eating fish for lunch and dinner. She told everyone in her office about it. Lo and behold, she did indeed begin to feel better. She looked better too: she smiled more and gained some needed weight, enough so that her colleagues commented on it.

In a month, though—after practically keeping the fishing industry afloat singlehandedly—Phyllis was ill again. The fish diet had not worked. All the excitement she had felt left her tired and embarrassed.

What was the value of hope for Phyllis? It did not cure her, but it gave her strength, some needed body weight, and one wonderful month. She suffered for several more years until she finally developed clearly defined lupus. She now controls her condition with medication and hopes for a cure in her future. Would she have given up those days of hope? "Never!" she says.

What Phyllis probably experienced was the placebo effect: A substance with no medical properties gave her a boost anyway, because she believed.

Feelings are chemical, says Bernie S. Siegel, M.D., author of the books *Love, Medicine and Miracles* (1987) and *Peace, Love and Healing* (1989), and a pioneer in psychoneuroimmunology, so called because it links our psychology with our nervous and immune systems. Take any group of people with symptoms, give them a sugar pill or some other harmless substance, and one out of three people will feel some relief from their symptoms because hope stimulates the release of our own endogenous painkiller, endorphin.

Doctors know all about the placebo effect, and many of them use it in addition to regular medicine. As one doctor said, "A third of my patients feel better if I just hold their hand."According to some studies, optimistic people live longer, and hospital patients with a fighting spirit are more likely to survive than patients who lie down and give up. You can probably tell some stories of your own!

A Suspended State of Hope

It is no coincidence that every religion celebrates the birth of a baby. Baptisms, showers, christenings, and circumcision ceremonies all tell us that a baby is the embodiment of hope.

> Sam's wife had just given birth to their third baby, a boy. They named him Carter. Nurses cleaned the tiny child, swaddled him in a soft pink-and-blue-striped receiving blanket, and handed him over to Sam. He looked down at Carter. No flaws yet! This tiny little being had his whole life ahead of him. A feeling of great hope swelled inside him.

For a new parent, the birth of a child is just the beginning of hope. Parents wish their children to be healthy, content, intelligent, and many other things, and they seem to wish for these things constantly. However, their desire is constantly peaking, diminishing, clicking off for short periods, then building again. It is impossible for most of us to live in a suspended state of hope.

Actually, long periods of hope can even be stressful. Think, for example, of those kinds of hope that never seem to end—we are in a hurry, but the hope lingers on and on. Our body is ready for action, and our mind is continually alert. This is the passion at its most exhausting.

Kris wanted Alan to ask her to marry him. She hoped Alan would ask. She hoped for years. She hoped so hard that her yearning craved action, but she waited. During the day, she daydreamed about life with Alan; at night, she dreamt about it. She decided to break up with him every year on her birthday. But she still had hope, so she stuck it out for another year . . . and another. Finally, after four and a half years, Alan produced a diamond ring. That night, Kris realized she felt really relaxed for the first time in years.

If hope becomes a reality, we can finally experience physical relief as well as psychological relief. When hope has no end in sight, our state of suspended anticipation eventually ends by itself.

Missing in action—that was how the army categorized Tom. Janet was determined not to accept this implied verdict that her husband had been killed in Vietnam. After all, her father had been missing in action. He had turned up emaciated and shellshocked but alive after six months in an enemy prison camp. Janet was so sure that Tom would return to her that the thought of giving up hope was impossible. She felt that her hope was keeping him alive.

Months passed, and still no Tom. A year passed; two years. Janet began to alternate between energizing hope and exhausting despair.

Suspended hope can end when something finally happens— either the dream becomes real or hope is extinguished for good. It can also end for no reason other than utter exhaustion.

A few special people are able to sustain hope for long times. These people add a few other factors to their hope to support it: faith, trust, a sense of their place in time.

The small nonprofit private school needed a piano. Enrollment was down, which led Dean Davis to feel that he should not buy a piano new from a store. Instead, he put out feelers. He mentioned his wish at meetings, to individual parents, and to others he thought would make likely benefactors. He knew that he would find a piano.

A year later, no piano had materialized. The dean did not give up hope. He believed that providence would provide the school with a piano in time.

Four years after he had first asked for a piano, Dean Davis received a phone call from a parent whose mother was moving to a nursing home. Would the school like to have her grand piano? The dean arranged for some piano movers—which the school could afford—right away!

The dean's hope had to wait, but this was not a discomfort or strain for him. Because of his beliefs, he was able to keep a low background hum of hope going for years.

Lost Hope

Lost hope is a common occurrence. It must be, because if all hopes came true, we would live in a very different world:

All lottery tickets would be big winners.
No business would go belly-up.
All vacations would be sunny and pleasant.
No car would be a lemon.
All children would grow into happy, fulfilled adults.
No teen would smoke her first cigarette.
All marriages would be harmonious.
No one would ever need a doctor.
All good deeds and hard work would be richly rewarded.

Our hopes are dashed constantly, for the world we live in is nothing like the one described above. Things go counter to our hopes all the time: It is as if fate borrows our hope and then hands it back to us broken, with no apologies. "Why?" we say. "Why me?" If we are extraordinarily flexible, we simply say, "Because that's life." *C'est la vie*—we hear it all the time.

Lost hope often feels like we have lost something real, but we must remember that we never really had the thing we lost. What we have lost is a dream. Dreams can always be born again in another time or another form.

The Hope Factory

Poet Alexander Pope reminded us three hundred years ago that hope springs eternal, and today's psychiatrists agree. Like joy, love, and other positive passions, you can make more hope if you know how.

You may feel that you could never be a person who creates hope. Hope does come more naturally to some of us than to others. Some of us have discovered hope as part of faith, love, or even desperation. Others of us were given the gift of hope by our parents.

The rest of us will have to give the gift of hope to ourselves. Many of us are afraid to hope. We try to protect against disappointment by hiding our hope from ourselves and others. But disappointment comes anyway! You may have lost your dream, and that is sad. But why lose the experience of hope as well? I am not asking you to leave the real world. I am asking you to recognize that in our real world, hope can make our daily life happier.·

Here is how you can learn to hope: act hopeful, look outward, look inward, focus on the positive, call up beautiful images, accept that your hope may never be real, assess the probability that your hope will become real, and borrow hope. Does this sound too simple? The truth is, all of these approaches work. The trick is to try them.

Act hopeful   Behave as if you are hopeful. Talk to others as if you are hopeful. Talk to *yourself* as if you are hopeful. Soon the world will react to you as if you are. Enjoy these hope experiences for themselves. Take pleasure in having your hope!

Look outward, look inward   In my Passions Survey, men and women generated hope the same ways, which came as something of a surprise. When I analyzed the respondents by age, though, a predictable pattern emerged: The younger people (in their twenties) tended to create hope by looking toward the future ("tomorrow is another day"), while the older ones (in their forties, fifties, and sixties) became introspective—they looked for silver linings, examined their own feelings, and sought wisdom from philosophers.

Focus on the positive   We are all very practiced at seizing on the passing negative—a criticism, an overheard conversation, an economic downturn, an omen—as information about our present and our future. But many of these negatives come to us through chance and error. To increase your quotient of hope, practice seizing on the passing positive—a compliment, the start of a new business or a new life, the momentary beauty of the season, a glimpse of life's worth. These positives can just as easily be signs of the future. Positive thinking brings immediate relief from hopelessness: We remind ourselves of reasons to go ahead with our lives, and soon our bodies are energized and in motion. Positive thinking also sets in motion self-fulfilling prophecies.

Is prayer positive thinking also? Sometimes it is, if we are praying for answers, guidance, or energy. Other kinds of prayer are deeply restful: We see ourselves in the perspective of the world, we get a realistic idea of what is possible, and we give up the remainder. We relax until we are rested and ready to move on. Prayer can put us in touch with a source of strength when we have no strength of our own. Soon the strength is in us again, and we can move toward our hope.

Call up beautiful images   Do not just feel—*visualize* what you hope for. Having a vision of hope in your mind is comforting, gives you a goal to reach for, and creates a reason to go on that you can see.

Accept that your hope may not lead to reality   Your hope may never come to pass. If you hope repeatedly for things that never come, you eventually will learn to retract your hope in order to avoid pain. To prevent damage to your capacity for hope, set your sights more realistically. Instead of banishing hope, become more realistic. You can always replace one hope with another, or take a break, then begin hoping again.

Borrow some hope from a friend   Take a lesson from someone with an outlook you admire. Does she deserve hope more than you do? Of course not. Is her life really better? She may be as familiar with sadness, loss, and helplessness as you are, or maybe she was in the past, at another time in her life, but look at her now! If her life really is better than yours, maybe it is because she is not afraid to allow herself to be uplifted by hope's possibilities, to take the wonderful chance that one day a dream might become a reality.

Hope's Forward March

It is amazing, when you think about it, that people hope at all. There is so much in our present to distract us and make us feel hopeless. People are cruel. Pollution, nuclear war, the greenhouse effect, drugs, AIDS . . . yet we look toward the future. Through our imaginations we can see past today's problems and give ourselves a great gift: a reason to go on. We imagine a better day. The hopeful among us are the survivors among us.

AWE: A Glimpse of the Infinite

Young people use the word *awesome* often, and they mean something is "terrific" or "great." But the word has another, much more powerful definition. Something awesome is something so wondrous and amazing that it is simply overwhelming.

We gasp; then breathing and our hearts seem to stop as time stands still. Goose bumps sweep over our body in a tidal rush, awareness sharpens to a knife point, we see newness in the old—it is amazing. We see mystery in the familiar, and we are immobilized by its power.

Did you know that the elderly report awe as frequently as children? Just as a child feels that the world is still a bit of a mystery, her grandparents are likely to feel that after all, the world is still a bit of a mystery. They are able to take a first look for the second time at the world around us. Perhaps this is why grandparents and grandchildren get along so well!

Did you know that feeling awe can be a sign of mental health? To experience awe, we must be able to pause for a moment. We must be able to give up our sense of control for a moment, must be able to focus on matters beyond ourselves for a moment. Think about it—you have come off the mountain, carried by the ski patrol, the doctors are working on a fractured bone in your leg—is this the moment that the mystery of your body is going to strike you? I think not. Or perhaps you can remember a time that you saved yourself and everyone in your car from disaster by swinging to your right and pumping the brake to avoid a collision. Is this the moment you're going to be flabbergasted by your visual-motor coordination and dexterity? I think not. To feel awe we must be able to relax, and we must have time enough to feel.

Did you know that it does not take extraordinary circumstances to inspire awe? It is the ordinary that awe focuses on most often. Yes, the depths of the ocean, the height and width of the universe, and the intricacies of the atom are awe-inspiring. But how often are we looking through a telescope, a microscope, or a glass-bottomed boat? It is that sensation of relief after the migraine passes, or the fact that something as splendid as angel food cake can come from combining eggs, sugar, flour, and air, or that you went to sleep with no introduction to your board presentation and came out of your morning shower with just the right words.

Awe is a mind and body emotion—a passion. But the potent ingredients of awe exist mainly in the mind. You may have noticed that the Passions Survey does not include questions about awe. It was only after we got the survey results back that we realized from the write-ins, the added notes, and later letters and interviews that awe was a major positive emotion that people wanted to talk about. Most of this chapter on awe comes from these write-ins, notes, interviews, and letters, as well as fifteen years of clinical experience.

Ingredient: Awareness

Have you ever read the child's book *Curious George*? It is about a monkey who touches things, picks up anything that is not nailed down, opens doors, plays with the telephone, explores the backs of trucks that are about to depart . . . and gets himself into all kinds of fixes. Nothing escapes the notice of this little monkey. Children love Curious George because he is so much like them! The human race would never have made any progress in understanding itself and the world if we had not been aware of the possibilities in the people, places, and things around us.

It is a shame that we have to tell a child in a store not to touch, or direct her attention to homework when she could play and learn on her own. Learning to discipline your mind and focus your thoughts is part of growing up, but that does not mean awareness of the whole world is squeezed out entirely. We must preserve our impulses to explore, to probe, to notice things, to be aware of everything.

If you feel you have lost these childlike qualities, did you know you can get them back? Welcome them consciously into your life. Set your own mental stage for them. Rather than accept everything you see, allow yourself to notice. Ask questions. Find out how things work, why they are here instead of there, and why the sky is blue. Look for colors and beauty, and prepare to be surprised.

Ingredient: Surprise

Surprise is often a precursor of awe. Surprise makes us pause and give awe a chance to happen. To be open to awe we must be open to surprise.

Most of us like surprises. Surprise is a delightful side effect of awareness and often an important part of awe. What is around the next corner? Is it new? Unexpected? Most of us enjoy the idea of not knowing everything, of always having a distant horizon to look to, of feeling the way a child feels again, that everything is new.

Seven-year-old Mark was grouchy. His mother had dragged him over to her friend's house to see a movie about a sick boy that might be shown later to Mark's scout troop. Mark found the movie boring. He refused to play with the toys his mother had brought along for him, sulked until the movie was over, then interrupted his mother frequently while she discussed the movie with her friend.

But this friend was wise in the way of children. While Mark whined, she crumpled up a piece of paper, squeezed it into a ball, and bounced it off his nose. He was quiet for a long five seconds. Then he began to laugh. Soon all three of them were laughing, and Mark behaved himself until it was time to leave.

If you are not feeling childlike or flexible, you may not be able to enjoy a surprise. In our adult world, worry and fatigue often interfere.

Cary had thought carefully about her boyfriend Ken's birthday. She knew he was interested in wine, so she made a reservation at a sophisticated wine bar they had intended to visit for some time. Her plan was to "kidnap" him out of work and transport him to the restaurant in a cab on the evening of his birthday.

Ken was not cooperative. "I'm tired," was all he said in the cab. The evening's conversation consisted of his talking about several dire situations in progress at the office. He did not like the wines they chose. Fifty-two dollars later, Cary promised herself she would never try to surprise this man again.

You may not be able to control other people's surprise reactions or nonreactions, but you can certainly make way for your own. The question is *how*, since you cannot actively place surprises in your own way. You can place yourself near the likely sites of surprises. If you stay home and see no one, chances are your life will not offer much in the way of surprise. The most you can expect is that the person who delivers your groceries will have tucked in a little extra something or maybe a TV show you watch will manufacture a surprise for you.

The best surprises come from people. People are unpredictable.

We change our minds, we change our looks, we buy gifts for no reason other than that we felt like it, we accomplish things we never thought we could. Children are eternally surprising. Most of all, we are playful—we enjoy surprising each other and do it on purpose. Magicians like it so much they make a life's work of it. For more surprise in your life, you will want more people in your life. People, as we shall see, are the source of several types of awe.

Ingredient: Pleasure

In most types of awe, we experience pleasure. This enjoyable sensation comes easily if we are already open to pleasurable experiences—if our life is oriented to focus on feeling the beautiful, the happy, the sensual, the positive. If we have forgotten about the pleasures of living, however, it can be hard to get awe off the ground.

Antony was too busy to feel anything except pressure since his daughters came to live with him. He had a project to complete at work, his two girls seemed unusually demanding, the housekeeper had just resigned, and dirty dishes and laundry were piling up. Antony was beginning to feel like one of the silver balls in a pinball machine: batted from side to side, launched on trajectories he could not control.

Saturday morning, the girls had plans to meet friends at the playground and he was the chauffeur. He parked, and the girls ran ahead down the shady path. Antony had walked this path a hundred times, but today he had a sensation he had not felt for weeks: He was finally alone. He stopped. The sun was strong on his skin; the trees edging the playground swayed in the breeze. He heard children's voices laughing and shouting. Every sensation was positively pleasurable, and he realized he had not felt pleasure for a long time.

Antony was now ready for awe. Sometimes, if we are lucky, pleasure can overtake us, as can surprise. Either can also help us make that necessary break with immediate problem solving, and become ready for awe.

Here are some of the variations on the theme that we can enjoy experiencing.

Awe of Accomplishment

The word for awe is probably "wow." In awe of an accomplishment, though, we often cannot speak at all. What we have just seen or experienced commands so much of our admiration that we do not want to spoil the moment with a distracting word. All of America was undoubtedly silent as Neil Armstrong set foot on the moon for the first time, or Nadia Comaneci competed for the Olympic gold, or the day the church bells rang because Dr. Jonas Salk had discovered the polio vaccine.

We can be in awe of our own achievements as well as those of others: You have just completed your first marathon. You lean against the wall, weak and in awe of what you have just done.

Awe can be found in the everyday as well as in the extraordinary performance. We take for granted that our hearts will beat and our lungs will draw breath, but to feel awe, all we need to do is pause a moment and ponder what *is*. Some awesome accomplishments took place in the past rather than in the present, and we can still appreciate their magnitude. The pacemaker, the television, the telephone, antibiotics—these inventions and discoveries were awesome in their time and still can be for us.

Awe of Beauty

The visual facets of life are an unequaled pleasure if we can be open to them. Children seem especially sensitive to some types of beauty.

Have you ever heard all the little voices go "ooh!" in unison when a large Christmas tree is lit?

Adults are susceptible to awe of beauty as well. We all enjoy the presence of a handsome specimen of the human race.

Carol and Laura were sitting together on the train when the door between the cars opened and someone walked in. They both glanced up and did a double take. The girl walking up the aisle was so flawlessly beautiful that Carol, Laura, and the rest of the passengers could not stop staring. The girl must have been used to it, because she smiled slightly. Carol and Laura looked at her as she came closer and passed by—not looking for faults but rather awed that anyone could carry beauty to such a transcendent level.

We can be in awe of inanimate objects as well. For example, a splendid musical composition or a work of art can evoke strong emotions:

Maude likes to tour large gardens because they are beautiful and offer surprises. She walks down a path, turns a corner, and sees . . . it could be anything from a lush wall of roses hanging heavily on a trellis to a sunny fountain inhabited by large goldfish to a grand sweep of lawn. One of Maude's most memorable experiences was her first visit to a walled Japanese garden. She gave a small contribution to the guard, he opened the door, she entered. Inside was a garden so beautifully designed, so impeccably tended, and so still that she too stood still while she glowed with appreciation.

Awe of Immensity

The world is large, we are small: This is something that children know and adults forget until they are reminded of it again. One woman enjoys traveling by ship because it gives her ample time to consider herself in relation to the sea. Here is an entry from her diary:

Location: the middle of the Atlantic Ocean. Nothing to see in any direction except water, sky, and the horizon where they meet, and nothing to do except sit in a deck chair and contemplate their bigness and our smallness. It is an occupation that can take hours, sometimes entire days.

The French say that everything in France is *très petit*, very small, and that in America, everything is *énorme*. It is not hard to justify some of those thoughts. New York's skyscrapers; the Great Lakes; the Rocky Mountains; the Grand Canyon; the West Coast—they can all be awe-inspiring. Says one Californian:

> Few driving experiences can equal the trip down the coast between San Francisco and Los Angeles. You drive at the very edge of amazing cliffs; ocean waves break far below, the sun glinting on the surface of the water far out to sea. This magnificent combination of land, sea, and sky goes on for miles, with endless variations as you drive along. The Park Service seems to have understood the nature of awe, because it has provided places to park so you can stop and look.

Fear is sometimes part of the awe of immensity. "It" is big and you are small. Enjoy the shift in perspective that awe brings and try to hold on to it after awe ebbs.

Awe of Nature

Natural beauty that is not immense can also be awe-inspiring. Surprise often helps to make it so.

> Dana was living in New York as an au pair girl in suburbia. Pretty homes on small, well-kept plots of land, and plenty of small parks, but nothing like Minnesota, she thought. Until, one day, she was driving her car along a busy avenue and turned off onto a narrow side street to avoid traffic. From there she turned on to

a smaller road, and that eventually became a dirt road. She headed up a crest—and stopped the car, stunned. Before her lay an enormous, placid lake, as big as anything she had ever seen back home. It was ringed by nature's most beautiful fall foliage. She felt tears come to her eyes.

Dana also felt an inner laugh beginning, a laugh of joy and surprise. She felt like laughing at herself, too, for now knowing that beauty could be found anywhere.

Awe of the Infinite

Most of us, most of the time, live within four walls. Once in a while we drive down a road where we can see far ahead. Occasionally, we stand near a window in a skyscraper or sit on a top of a mountain and look into the distance all the way to a flat horizon. We hardly ever look up at the sky and the stars to feel an awe of the infinite.

The astronomy instructor had told her class that the meteor shower would be spectacular, and she offered some specific locations on campus where the viewing would be good. As it happened, Jody's dorm room was better than them all: The modern windows spanned one wall, and the view was in the right direction.

Jody set her alarm for midnight, got up, washed her face, and sat down in the chair she had pulled near the window before she went to bed. She stared into the darkness for sixty seconds and saw nothing. Then—a motion, and she caught a glimpse of a shooting star as it faded. Then another, and another. She felt goose bumps starting. Some of the meteors were bright balls that lasted quite a long time compared to others. She stopped trying to follow the meteors with her eyes—she was catching them all after a while, and in a constant state of goose bumps. It was 2 A.M. before she knew it.

Some people experience awe in their dreams. Jessica was about to turn thirty-five. She knew all the thoughts you were supposed to have about birthdays: regrets about missed opportunities, about lines on your face, about gray hairs and changing body contours. She did not experience those feelings very intensely and was surprised when her real feelings revealed themselves to her the night before her birthday.

Jessica was floating in black space, far above the earth, far from any place at all. All worries were contained in some distant world; here was total peace and comfort. Nothing to see, hear, or feel. *Being* was the only sensation.

In the quiet darkness, Jessica saw a point of golden light. The point began to grow into a circle, and soon she could see that it was spinning slowly around. Jessica watched in complete awe. A little piece of the circle spun off and began to grow into its own circle of light; slowly, silently, a piece eddied off that one, until there were nine gold lights in a row, spinning quietly, existing with her. She felt as if she had witnessed the creation of the universe and awoke exhilarated and joyful.

Jessica's true feelings about birthdays were that they are among the most awesome occasions people celebrate. The beginning of a life—what could be filled with more hope and love? Jessica probably was out of touch with those feelings because society rarely reinforces them. Her dream reminded her that her life was far from over and that a life-giving awe was still a part of her.

Religious Awe

In many religions, we give ourselves over to a greater whole, a spirit that we are just a part of. If we are open to this idea, we do not need to be in a church or synagogue to feel religious awe. Awe is an experience that depends on *perception*, how you see things. Neil felt it in his living room.

Neil was sitting on the couch, enjoying the peace and gentle natural light of the gray winter's day. He looked out the window and was struck by the fact that not a single leaf on the deep green privet hedge was moving. It was absolutely still.

One of the holiday cards he had propped up on his desk near the window caught Neil's eye. Though it was a nighttime snow scene, the card looked very bright—it even seemed to have a hazy ring of light around it. Neil got up and went over to the card. It said, "Listen to the stillness. God is at work." Neil felt awed and can still recapture that feeling of oneness with the world when he remembers the experience.

Once upon a time, *awe* was a religious word—it meant a reverential fear and dread. God was the source of all awe. Many people see God's presence in all of the awe-inspiring experiences we have today: in accomplishment, beauty, nature, immensity, the infinite, and the everyday.

In Search of Awe

You do not have to look to the immense or the mystical to find awe. Everyday occurrences can be just as awesome: a new person is born—that has been called the "everyday miracle." A small child masters a complicated memory game, someone sings with a magnificent voice or plays an instrument and it moves you . . . a medication makes you feel better, a spider spins a web. There is awe in the minuscule as well as in the immense, awe in the everyday as well as in the extraordinary, if only you can see it.

Seeing—that is the thing. Amazing people, places, experiences, accomplishments, and natural beauty are all around us, but we often do not take the time to notice them. We do not understand our relationships with other people or appreciate our world. Your relationships and your world will roll along fine without your appreciation, but what if you *did* try to approach them? You would understand more about your place and your appreciation would grow. You might even decide that *you* are incredibly magnificent. You are, you know.

To recapture awe and increase your awe quotient (A.Q.), you need to:

Take time out Try tacking on time-outs after each meal. Since meals tend to come at least three times a day, you've automatically scheduled at least three time-outs a day. Sit for an extra minute or two. Complete the following sentence: Isn't it amazing that _____ . Or try this sentence: I am filled with wonder when I think of _____ . Or perhaps: I never before noticed _____ . Not only are you more likely to begin to feel bits and pieces of awe, but you will have those experiences to share with others and perhaps build their A.Q. also.

Other ways, times, and places to find awe: Gaze out the window on the train. Look around in the waiting room at the doctor's office. Sit on the porch or balcony. Use your eyes, ears, nose, skin, and taste buds to take in the fullness of your surroundings.

Allow yourself to be amazed To feel joy, love, and hope, you must relax the ties of your thoughts and let feeling wash over you. Awe is no different—in fact, there is more letting go here than in any of the other emotions, because you are losing yourself in the awesome object. It becomes important; you are the powerless observer. If this makes you uncomfortable, remember that it lasts only a moment. It will be one of the richest moments of your life if you allow yourself to let it carry you away.

Imagine life without To feel awe for what we have, start taking things away. What was it like before we had electric lights? How did we ever get along without vitamins? What if there were no such thing as an orchestra or even music? What if plants never flowered? Imagining the nonexistence of such things can deepen appreciation.

Practice sensate focus   In sex therapy, sensate focus means becoming fully receptive to all the pleasurable sensations your partner is providing. We can focus on all of the pleasurable sensations that the world provides. We have five finely tuned sensory capacities which we can develop more: the capacities to see, hear, touch, taste, smell.

The most developed of these is the visual. Imagine yourself a camera. Scan the people, places, things, and nature in your life. What do you see through the viewfinder? If you do not find anything beautiful or amazing, try a close-up focus. Keep looking; wait and try again.

Now use your ears and focus only on the sensations coming in. It is amazing that so many sounds can bombard you at once, and yet you can focus on the sound of music, a voice, a bird.

Think about the scent of the air—fragrances of perfume or flowers, food aromas, the different smells of houses . . . Researchers have found that our sense of smell is a powerful trigger for memories and that aromas can help us relax or make us feel better. Some smells are good, some are bad, some are neutral; all are part of the experience of the moment. Their sheer power can lift and shift you from the ordinary everyday life into extraordinary awe.

Wonderful tastes—these too can contribute to awe. The delicate blend of spices in pumpkin pie, the pleasant burn of seasoned Chinese food, a delectable pastry . . . how surprising it is that such different, delightful flavors exist at all! And we are finding or creating new ones all the time.

The largest organ on the body is skin. It is filled with nerve endings that are sensitive to pressure, heat, cold, vibration, flutter, or combinations of those sensations. Our sense of touch brings us information about the outside world and also about our inner world. It can tell us that we are energized, sleepy, and hungry. We can feel each other through our sense of touch (remember touch is important—the infant who is not touched will die). Focus on what your skin is sensing.

Now, experience all five senses working at once. Does this give you a feeling of awe? If not, start again.

Do not confuse awe with fleeting moments   Awe may be momentary, but its hallmark is a cognitive restructuring which lasts and lasts. *Cognition* is thinking; *restructuring* refers to new views. Together these terms tell us that seeing or thinking in a new way or finding an old view anew gives us feelings that are new or rediscovered anew.

Mark and Mark Jr. were not getting along well. It had gotten much worse, Mark thought, when Mark Jr. had become old enough to drive. They battled over car rights, curfew times, his hair, his friends. Mark was beginning to worry that he did not love or even like his own son.

Then Mark began to remember how he had felt when he was eighteen years old. He realized his son was doing something very normal: He was growing up. Mark Jr. wanted to take some of his own risks rather than hear about risks from old Dad. He wanted to find out about the world on his own. Mark suddenly realized that Mark Jr. was a man. He noticed how big Mark Jr. was, how strong, how assertive—how attractive to girls, too. He was amazed his son had come so far.

An experience of awe is one that may change us for life. Mark's father will never be able to see his son as a child again: That is the new comprehension his awe brought him. In the years to come, researchers will probably learn a great deal more about exactly how this rush of understanding rearranges paths and structures within the brain. It will be fascinating.

Making the move into awe readiness is not difficult. There is less to fear here than you may think: we expect the awe to end, and we know we can carry the experience with us in our memory almost intact, so we need not fear that the passing of awe will be sad. Its chemicals influence the mind more than the body, so physical withdrawal is painless as well. We need not worry that we will hurt anyone or ourselves, because awe is sheer pleasure for all involved.

Our moments of awe are precious to us because they are the moments when we are most alive, when we see most clearly who we are and the beauty of the world around us. This purifying passion can make us feel as if we have been reborn. That is the promise of awe: a new view of a brand-new world.

EPILOGUE

Most of us feel we are comfortable with our emotions the way they are. We think that we are exactly as emotional as is natural. We each feel different amounts of joy, love, awe, hope, rage, fear, despair, or guilt, and these feelings are as personal as a fingerprint.

It is hard to imagine that our emotional lives could need more texture or fine-tuning when we are so used to them, but as we have seen, it is often just what we need.

If every aspect of your life—your work, home, family, finances—is intolerable, you have everything to gain by exploring your emotions and nothing to lose. If you are crying every day for reasons you do not understand, if your appetite for food or for living are gone, if you are an alcoholic whose last friend has just walked away, you may be on the brink of reaching out for a transformation. Many people say they cannot embrace a positive emotion or rid themselves of constant negativity until they have nothing left to lose. Until they reach that point, the risk of taking life into their own hands and failing is too great. It is not until they *must* take the chance that they find the strength they need.

Or perhaps your life may have no such noticeable drama—you simply feel, deep inside, that you want a fuller life. A small voice says that there could be more. Listen to yourself! By exploring your emotions, you can be like the phoenix, the fabulous mythical bird that survives the fire and rises out of the ashes even more beautiful than before. Your face will have more character, your step more stamina. Your spiritual focus will be clearer. Your empathy will be deeper because your emotional experience will be more textured and varied.

One of the biggest misconceptions that slows down this rebirth is our tendency to blame ourselves for our own faults. Women, especially, feel embarrassed, shamed, and guilty when bad things happen. We feel we must endure our negative passions because we deserve them; we believe we have no right to positive passions.

It is far more accurate to see all of the woes that befall us as inconveniences, not personalized messages from hell. You can deal with inconveniences by going around them, climbing over them, sliding under them, or getting out your emotional crowbar and prying them out of the way. Acknowledge that negative passions are part, but not all, of life. Then embrace and create the positive passions.

Passions are part of us. We are preprogrammed to feel them. Escape is impossible. Accepting passions, welcoming them, embracing them, and letting them be is a way of uniting parts of ourselves. Once we understand them, we can delicately turn down the volume of the passions we do not enjoy and amplify the passions we prefer.

The turning point comes when you stop looking at yourself from the outside—you stop focusing on what other people think—and start looking at the outside world from inside. If you have been hurt by human frailty or random tragedy—this change in the way you see yourself and the world is critical. This is when you will stop looking for someone else to save you and begin to draw on your own inner strength. Therapists, doctors, clergypeople, and family can help you, but to rise again—like the phoenix—you must also use your own intuitive feelings, common sense, courage, and intelligence to rebuild.

Hug yourself. Hold your own hand. Parent yourself. Even if you were not born lucky or beautiful or wealthy or courageous, you can be born again by listening to, acknowledging, and acting upon your passions.

APPENDIX
Where to Get Help

This appendix gives you many choices once you feel ready to look for help. At each center or organization, you will find people who will not be surprised by your problem and who will know how to assist you.

It's best to make an appointment with each organization before planning a visit. Many will send you printed information.

To Find a Therapist

The American Psychiatric Association; the American Psychological Association; the National Association of Social Workers; the National Mental Health Association; and the American Association of Marriage and Family Therapists have branches in nearly every state. (Look in the white pages of your telephone directory under county or state names if you don't find them under "American" or "National.")

For certified pastoral counselors, write to the American Association of Pastoral Counselors, 9504A Lee Highway, Fairfax, VA 22031.

Alcohol and Drug Dependency

Hazelden, Box 11, Center City, MN 55012. (612) 257–4010. Private residential treatment program. Individual and group therapy.

Betty Ford Center, 39000 Bob Hope Drive, Rancho Mirage, CA 92270. 1–(800) 392–7540 (out of state, 1–(800) 854–9211). Typical stay is twenty-eight days. Includes an outpatient program.

Women's Alcoholism Center, 2261 Bryant Street, San Francisco, CA 94110. (415) 282–8900. Residential program for low-income women with children. Includes drug abuse counseling. Six-month minimum stay for non-working women. Also outpatient program.

Alcohol and Drug Treatment Center at Stanford Medical Center, Department of Psychiatry, Room TF104, Stanford, CA 94305. (415) 723–6682. Offers extensive outpatient care and in-hospital detoxification.

Foley House, 10511 Mills Avenue, Whittier, CA 90604. (213) 944–7953. Residential program for twenty women can take ten children. A thirty- to ninety-day program but can be up to six months.

Women's Alcoholism Program, 6 Camelia Avenue, Cambridge, MA 02139. (617) 661–1316. Also treats drug addictions. Outpatient program includes group therapy.

WomanPlace, 11 Russell Street, Cambridge, MA 02140. Inpatient care for alcohol and drug abuse.

Gosnold on Cape Cod, 200 TerHeun Drive, Falmouth, MA 02540. (617) 540–6550. Includes Gosnold Treatment Center (inpatient); Gosnold Counseling Center (outpatient); Stephen Miller House (for men); and Emerson House (for women). Extended care for adult women, pregnant women, adolescents.

Gateway Rehabilitation Center, Moffett Run Road, Aliquippa, PA 15001. 1–(800) 472–1177 (out of state, 1–(800) 472–4488). Typical stay twenty-eight days. Has more than ninety beds.

South Oaks Hospital, Alcoholism Program and Substance Abuse and Addictions Service, 400 Sunrise Highway, Amityville, NY 11701. 1–(800)–732–9808. Inpatient and outpatient care. Also offers referral service.

Arms Acres, Alcoholic Rehabilitation Program, PO Box X, Seminary Hill Road, Carmel, NY 10512. 1–(800)–227–2767 (out of state, 1–(800) 431–1268). In-hospital residential treatment for alcohol and cross-addiction.

Mountainwood, 500 Old Lynchburg Road, P.O. Box 5546, Charlottesville, VA 22905. 1–(800)–899–8245. Residential program. Can take up to 140 patients. Offers treatment programs designed especially for women, adolescents, Vietnam vets.

The following organizations operate networks, with treatment programs across the country:

Parkside Medical Services, Park Ridge, IL. (708) 698–4730.

Mediplex Group, Koala Centers, West Palm Beach, FL. (407) 655–9300.

Women for Sobriety, Quakertown, PA. (215) 536–8026.

Alcoholics Anonymous, New York, NY. (212) 686–1100.

The following groups offer hotlines and referrals:

National Institute on Drug Abuse, Rockville, MD. 1–(800)–662–HELP.

The National Cocaine Hotline: 1–(800)–COCAINE.

Woman to Woman (run by the Junior League), New York, NY. (212) 355–4380 (in New York State, 1–(800) ALCALLS).

National Council on Alcoholism and Drug Dependence, Inc., New York, NY. (212) 206–6770.

Cocaine Anonymous, Culver City, CA. (213) 839–1141.

Smoking

There are various methods used in many different types of programs available for those who want to quit smoking. It's best to do some research and decide what's best for your particular situation. The following organizations can refer you to local chapters or provide you with information on what's available in your area:

American Cancer Society, 1–(800) ACS–2345. Two-week programs within a support group.

American Lung Association, 1740 Broadway, New York, NY 10019. (212) 315–8700. Twenty-day self-help program.

American Heart Association, 7320 Greenville Avenue, Dallas, TX 75231. (214) 373–6300. Provides information.

Eating Disorders

The following organizations offer treatment. Check for cost and any specific requirements for admission.

American Health and Diet Company, 475 Park Avenue South, New York, NY 10016. (212) 223–0833 (out of state, 1–(800) 828–7017). Conducts workshops and offers referral service.

Gracie Square Hospital Eating Disorders Program, 420 East 76th Street, New York, NY 10021. (212) 222–2832 (out of state, 1–(800) 382–2832). Offers consultations, referrals, and an inpatient program.

The Renfrew Center, 475 Spring Lane, Philadelphia, PA 19128. (215) 482–5353. Also, 7700 Renfrew Lane, Coconut Creek, FL. (305) 698–9222. Both are forty-bed facilities in estate settings; offer residential treatment for women. Forty-five- to sixty-day program.

Johns Hopkins Medical Institutions Eating Disorders Clinic. Meyer Building, 600 North Wolfe Street, Baltimore, MD 21205. (301) 955–3863. Inpatient and outpatient treatment. Average stay is thirty days, with aftercare.

UCLA Neuropsychiatric Institute Eating Disorders Program, 760 Westwood Plaza, Los Angeles, CA 90024. (213) 825–5730. Offers inpatient and outpatient treatment.

University of Cincinnati Medical Center Eating Disorders Clinic, University of Cincinnati, Cincinnati, OH 45267–0559. (513) 558–5118. Four-week residential program.

The following organizations provide information and referrals for treatment in your area:

National Anorexic Aid Society (NAAS), 1925 East Dublin Granville Road, Columbus, OH 43229. (614) 436–1112.

American Anorexia and Bulimia Association. 418 East 76th Street, New York, NY 10021. (212) 734–1114.

Anorexia and Bulimia Resource Center, 225 Alhambria Circle, Suite 321, Coral Gables, FL 33134. (305) 444–3731.

Sexual Addictions

It is best to check with your local chapter of Alcoholics Anonymous for information on groups in your area that use the AA methods to help sexual addictions. There are some Sexaholics Anonymous chapters in major cities.

The American Association of Sex Educators, Counselors and Therapists will also help guide you to a certified sex therapist or group therapy appropriate to your problem. Contact them in Washington, D.C., at 11 Dupont Circle, NW, Suite 220, Washington DC 20036–1207.

The Society for Sex Therapy and Research can also provide referrals. Contact them through Leonore Tiefer, Ph.D., Department of Urology, Montefiore Medical Center, Bronx, NY 10467. (212) 920–4576.

ABOUT THE AUTHOR

GEORGIA WITKIN, PH.D., has a private clinical practice
and is an assistant clinical professor in the department
of psychiatry at Mount Sinai School of Medicine in
New York City. She has appeared as a guest expert on
over one hundred television programs, including *Don-
ahue, The Oprah Winfrey Show, 20/20, Today, Good Morning America,* and *Hour Magazine.* Her comments and
articles have appeared on the pages of numerous pub-
lications, including *USA Today* and *Time* magazine.